eat well ~ feel well

eat well ~ feel well
Slow cooking in a short while

Julian Barker

AEON

First published in 2024 by
Aeon Books

British Library Cataloguing in Publication Data

A C.I.P. for this book is available from the British Library

ISBN-13: 978-1-80152-136-9

Typeset by Medlar Publishing Solutions Pvt Ltd, India

www.aeonbooks.co.uk

*to the many
who have nourished me
and for those I have fed*

CONTENTS

PREFACE

Elizabeth David, doyenne of postwar English cookery writers, collected a number of recipes centred around Le Creuset cookware in a small wire–bound booklet, published by the company in 1969. The recipes I present in this booklet differ entirely from hers, as does their intention. But I cannot resist quoting from her introductory remarks:

> Some of the very first cooking utensils I ever owned were orange–red cast–iron casseroles lined with white enamel. They took my fancy ... during a pre–war trip to France ... they did much to help me ... everything I cooked seemed to turn out right. They were cheerful and clean–looking ... saved me washing up ... looked civilised on the table. My affection for them grew.

By the time she had written this little piece, she had made her reputation with *French Provincial Cookery* and had opened a shop in Pimlico where I bought some of my own pots and pans. I agree with her entirely about the cookware but I am hoping to address a wider audience with an especial interest in suggesting a small but rich repertoire of tasty good food for working families with children. But everyone needs to eat well to feel well.

NOTICE

The author has received no payment or payment in kind or promotional advantage from any of the producers or suppliers of cookware mentioned in this book.

Health from an enjoyable diet

This is a book about self-care. We all need to eat and enjoy our food. In home cooking, any blending can be done by hand rather than by machine. Baby food has to be relatively smooth but adults need to eat their solids. That marks the end of my campaign against smoothies.

This is a workaday guide rather than a fancy cookery book: there are no recipes for dinner-parties or other entertainment: there are more than enough of those already. This is about good living for self and family rather than display for others. But guests will be impressed.

I have kept it methodical and simple which is all you need if you want to feed yourself and family all year round. I have not invented a "method", just a way of doing things well and satisfyingly. It is slow-cooking for families and people in a hurry. Slow cooking but in a short while is quiet and sure. It preserves nutrients and flavour and keeps the temperature low so the health benefits of cold-pressed olive oil are not lost to heat.

The emphasis of the method is on breakfast but there are also plenty of straightforward recipes for lunch and dinner. Enough for a fortnight.

Each of us grew up in a food culture. The great profusion of foods in our shops and confusion of information from our media may loosen this anchor to our wellbeing and make it possible for our inherent sense of food to be dispersed. If this book was all you had as a source of information, I can guarantee that you would at least have the opportunity to be healthily well–fed.

The appendix on foods broadens out the information embodied in the recipes where the health benefits of each ingredient of the breakfasts is detailed. Just in case you have any interest in the broad science of nutrients I have given a summary tucked away at the back of the book.

Cooking, like gardening, involves standing and a lot of movement so is very good exercise and, unlike going to the gym, will benefit others as well as you.

Benefits

The great advantage of doing things this way is that children get fed well before they start their day. A cooked breakfast anchors their health, their attention span and their capacities for the day ahead: they (and you) will have protein, fats, carbohydrates in a meal rich in minerals and vitamins.

Other great advantages provided by this simple way of cooking:

1. Washing-up is easier and there will be less of it.
2. Less fuel is used. I suspect food waste would be reduced.
3. Foods in these recipes are not only nutrient–dense but full of flavour. Flavour is itself a nutrient.
4. Less hurry and heat in the kitchen means less stress for everyone. The food is not fried but gently braised. The health benefits of olive oil and butter (reduced by frying) are therefore retained.
5. The pans I recommend retain heat so that food remains warm but not over–cooked should anyone delay coming to eat. No need to warm the plates.
6. This is neither frying nor grilling but slow–cooking in a short while …

Total cooking time for breakfast:
typically 20–40 minutes

but only a small part of that is spent in the kitchen
because slow–cooking looks after itself

Although not vegetarian,
the focus of the suggestions in this book emphasise:
plant foods and herbs
and the great value and taste in the process of:
steaming ⇔ resistant starch ⇔ vegetable stock
(details later)

Cooking

For those fortunate to witness it when young, there is no mystique. You just know that, with a little attention, the everyday magical transformation of raw ingredients into cooked food as an act of care for self and others is possible, necessary and desirable. For those who experience anxiety about "being able" to cook, just remind yourself that there are only a few simple guidelines which anyone can follow; I hesitate to call them "rules":

1. Assemble all the ingredients before you start or at least know for certain that they are close to hand. Rummaging about at the last moment ruins your peace of mind, converts calm into stress and may spoil the food.
2. Invest in a range of good steel, glass and cast-iron ceramic cookware. They will cost a good deal of money but you will only have to do this once in your lifetime and your heirs will be grateful to receive them.
3. Give house room only to very good sharp knives. Blunt knives, besides being frustrating and a source of stress in the kitchen, are dangerous: they slip. Sharp knives do not slip and by giving them a brief caress with the sharpener, you will have preloaded care and attention into your working mind. So, make sure that you have

at least three good knives—small, medium, large—and a sharpening stone. You just draw the blade at an angle on each side in turn. That's it.

4. Starting with a cluttered and messy working space makes for stressful cooking and is a false economy of time not to have cleared up before you begin. Whenever I ignore this precept, I pay for it in one way or another.

5. You can cook many meals in ten minutes but the recipes in this book suggest that you allow half an hour. The method is detailed on the section on BREAKFAST, one for each weekday.

6. If you are rushed in the morning or children have to be got ready for school, much can be done the night before. When I was on duty, I preferred to get up earlier instead so that they were fed before they had to rush out the door (but am glad that I am not called upon to do it again)!

Breakfast cereals are cheap and easy and get around all these time constraints. But at what cost to your health? They did not in our household ever stand in for a cooked breakfast. Porridge may work well as a breakfast starter but is insufficient on its own

Although, in theory, you might ideally want twenty minutes to let a meal go down well after eating, for families and working people, that advice is unrealistic and will often just have to be overlooked. At least, rushing out the door on a full belly makes a powerful contrast with doing the same on an empty stomach.

Confidence

Those who are already confident and capable cooks may know and take for granted all that I have said thus far, but they may have learnt at an early age. It is easy to gloss over the obvious or avoid stating it for fear of seeming to patronise, but any skill depends upon some very simple routine which has to be acquired. Once routines become a part of daily practice, they stick in the way you hope your food won't. So this book does a good deal of stating the obvious. But something is only obvious once you have done it and so know how.

In my own case, I was considered a good instinctive cook from my late teens to my early twenties, but, looking back, that reputation—such as it was—depended upon a carefree manner that concealed the use of expensive ingredients and a very careful reading of fashionable recipes. All right if you want to be flash but in the intervening years before having a family, I lost whatever confidence and skill I might have gained and then, on account of being responsible for the nourishment of others, I returned to the pans of my youth and taught myself how to make better use of their special properties.

Of course, we could always rely on the division of labour and live with a person who is kitchen–capable, but it is good to share and enjoy the pleasure in seeing others well-fed (and on occasion their appreciation)! Also, as self–reliance is good for self–esteem, it helps to have a simple, structured, stressless method to build confidence in the rudiments of looking after oneself. That is what this book is about but once you have established or modified your own routines, it will have served its purpose.

Misplaced confidence

I had the misplaced confidence to apply to cook breakfast in a bijou hotel in Notting Hill (after all, I had washed up in The Singing Chef— trendy in 1963—and had even tossed some frozen prawns into a pan). I had mistaken the confidence (and what then passed for brio) in TV chef Philip Harben as a sign of knowledge. He taught me all I didn't know. A young American guest at the hotel ordered an (expensive) omelette so, of course, I was the man. She barely touched it, to my lasting shame. I set about learning by doing and hope you will trust the practicality of this book.

What do you need?

Pans, a wooden spoon or two and very few other implements (no need for gadgets that take up space and depend upon an electric motor) and a gas hob with preferably an electric oven.

Pans

Cast-iron enamelled pans with their well-fitting lids distribute heat evenly and retain moisture with flavour and nutrients.

Glass is also excellent if a little less versatile but is lighter. The glass casserole I bought more than twenty years ago still does the best roast chicken, though I prefer cast iron for lamb. I do not use any non–stick products[1] and have never used a micro–wave.

---

[1] On account of their incorporation of Polytetrafluoroethylene (PTFE). There are more than enough toxic chemicals in the environment.

Pans for breakfast

1. Pyrex™ or CorningWare™ small glass saucepan with lid
2. Le Creuset shallow casserole with close–fitting lids:
   - 22 cms for one or two people
   - 26 cms for three or four people (or two with large appetites)
   - 30 cms for four or six people

Casseroles for roasts and stews

1. Large Pyrex™ or CorningWare™ glass rectangular casserole with lid
2. I have also found small round glass casseroles by CorningWare™ very good for cooking vegetables in the oven and for food storage; they are in American sizes and mine come out in metric to 0.9 and 1.4 litres as well as a handsome red oval one at 1.9 litres
3. Le Creuset enamelled cast–iron round or oval casserole, or
4. Le Creuset oval doufeu

The great advantage of such pots: they save you from faffing about with domes of foil to cover a roast on a baking tin: you just have a solid well–fitting lid to place on or lift off as you please.

Other pans

It is good to have an iron or a stainless steel frying pan (preferably both) if you need to speed things up occasionally. Although I have some ancient iron pans, one of the most versatile is stainless steel: designed by Michel Roux. I suppose it is a kind of sauté pan. It has deep curved sides, so operates both as saucepan and slow frying pan (and I happen to have a lid that fits): its solid base means that food doesn't get over-heated or anywhere near charred even if you turn up the heat to hurry things along a little. As excellent as it is, the base is too small and the sides too tall for French omelettes; if you want to make these best to reserve a pan just for them [see Thursday Breakfast].

Steamer

To retain nutrient and texture[2] it is better never to put vegetables in water but above boiling water, in a steamer.

The bottom pan that holds the boiling water will become your *stockpot* which can hold one or two or even more steamer pans stacked above it. This water will become one of your essential cooking ingredients, your Vegetable Stock. [For details see section on *Other Meals* which follows the breakfast recipes]

Tools

- Wooden spoons and spatulas are essential. I have also managed to find some nice wooden dining spoons. They seem to enhance the flavour of food and helps avoid scratching enamel with knives.
- At least one slotted spoon will be needed, metal or wooden or both. It seems that they are designed for caterers and you cannot get a small one which would suit the home kitchen very well.[3]
- You'll probably want a metal spatula (so-called fish slice) though wooden ones work just as well. No need for ugly silicone which I wouldn't trust near food once they start to disintegrate.
- There are some dishes and situations when food tongs work much better than spatulas and spoons. Some are constructed like scissors with a hinge in the middle while others have a hinge at the end; best to have one of each.

    None of the recipes in this book call for any motorised implements.
- If you want to make wonderful nutritious gravy (without a sticky, poorly digestible roux which is a fuss to make) you will be well served by the conical solid metal strainer known as a chinois. [See Sunday roast Chicken.]
- To reduce this kind of rich semi-solid mixture into delicious semi-liquid gravy you will also need a good masher which will double

---

[2] And to form resistant starch which has a section to itself later.
[3] It so happens I found two such wooden slotted spoons, one dessertspoon sized, the other a large teaspoon in a street market in Lithuania but no entrepreneur, to my knowledge, has thought of large-scale manufacture in metal or wood. My dainty olive ladle is just too small.

well for mashed potatoes. I have two: a simple one and a very clever one from Jamie Oliver.

Other necessities

The following will make life in the kitchen more enjoyable on a daily basis without taking up too much space. Even the smallest kitchen could accommodate them and I have been known to go camping equipped with most of these:

- A set of Pyrex glass measuring jugs, at least one each of:
  ➤ small (¼ litre),
  ➤ pint (just over ½ litre) and
  ➤ one litre.
  These jugs are sort of stackable, ideal to store stock made from the water from the steamer pan. They double up well as mixing bowls. I also have a larger jug (about 5 litres) but as I use it infrequently (for instance at Christmas), you may not want to give house room to such a big one.
- Glass or china mixing bowls. You will need at least a couple of these (they stack anyway) for putting leftovers in the fridge (covered by a plate) and for chopped ingredients if you don't like sending them straight from the chopping board into the pan. Although I like to use a nice earthenware bowl with a spout for beating and pouring eggs, just as often a large cup that has lost its handle serves perfectly well. Avoid plastic and ban cling-film from the house. These are endocrine disruptors (as are bowls and cups from which washing up liquid has not been rinsed): bad for you and bad for the environment.
- Wooden chopping boards: don't be persuaded by glass or plastic. Although small ones are good for chopping herbs, ingredients that don't always stay put call for a bigger size and less fiddling about. A large chopping board will double for making and eating a sandwich snack, or for serving cheese or omelette.
- One or two wire hand whisks. Eggs should have their very own, keeping a separate one for milk and gravies.
- A sprouter if you want to make your own bean sprouts. In theory, you could use a set of old jam jars with muslin but in practice they take up too much space and use up more time. A bean–sprouter is nothing more than a stack of perforated trays. The wholefood shop

that sells them will probably also stock a good quality of the seeds to sprout. You can buy them already made but they go off quite quickly and are never so good as your own.

- A grater of some sort. I use a microplane when I have a big chunk of parmesan but for smaller pieces *Zyliss* do very good rotary hand–graters.
- A couple of colanders (or three) and a wire strainer
- A salad spinner (or two): I use a small one for washing and drying fresh parsley which fits inside the larger one for salad leaves. In theory, you could instead improvise with colanders and tea towels but in practice they are fiddly, more time–consuming and very unsatisfactory.
- You will probably already have a pair of big heavy scissors. A small but strong pair do very well for snipping chives or parsley directly onto food. Saves getting out the chopping board.
- A couple of skewers.

This book is not about baking which I believe calls for more implements. I am lucky to have a local artisan bakery: I leave everything to them.

Heat

These recipes (if you can even call them that) are designed for gas hobs.[4] My own has solid cast iron pan supports with 4 burners with the following characteristics:

Medium 70 mm burner	Medium 70 mm burner
Large 100 mm burner	Small 55 mm burner

Apart from omelettes for which you can use the large, the foods in the book call for small and medium burners.

---

[4] Gas is the perfect fuel for cooking on hobs and these pots and dishes make the best use of it. Burning excessive amounts of it cannot of course be condoned but this book promotes using it at a minimum and electricity for ovens where gas would be inefficient and wasteful and not produce such good results.

Cooking speeds

1	Ultra–fast	Searing food	Up to half a minute
2	Fast	Frying food in oil or fat	One to four minutes
3	Intermediate	Slow frying with a lid	Up to ten minutes
4	Fairly slow	Braising food under a lid	Ten–25 minutes
5	Slow	Braising or stewing	40–75 minutes
6	Very Slow	Roasting or stewing	1½–3 hours

The breakfast recipes in this book concentrate on speeds 3 and 4.

Apart from French omelettes, I don't recommend searing food …

If eggs spend longer than 30 seconds in the pan before being turned onto a plate, they cease to be French omelettes and become in effect fast fried eggs.

Occasionally you may want to speed things up but this is not really a book about fried food. Frying and sautéing[5] gives you the pleasure of caramel but loses subtle flavours and nutrients. The great health benefits of olive oil are lost once its smoke point is exceeded. This fact perhaps more than any other spurred on the popularity of cooking with coconut fat (marketed as "oil").

---

[5] Like frying but typically with higher heat, less oil and stirring the food vigorously.

"Breakfast like a king, lunch like a prince, dine like a pauper"

I have heard this saying in each of the countries I have visited which number more than a few. In Russia, they tell me, the variant on this advice says: "give your dinner to your enemy"! The idea suggests that a substantial preferably cooked breakfast will set you up for whatever the day might bring. Front-loading a day's intake of food and tapering it off in the evening provides another benefit: it will also make for better quality of sleep. The regal breakfast is rich in all five classes of nutrient: protein, fat, carbohydrate, minerals and vitamins, which is what my recipes will give you.

Overview of the basic breakfast approach
[details under daily recipes]

1. Light the gas at its lowest setting beneath the shallow casserole or glass saucepan on a small or medium ring. Add a dessertspoonful of extra virgin olive oil
2. Add chopped foods and herbs in stages

   With this method you can leave the kitchen for ten minutes or so to get ready for the day or attending to small people or other tasks, returning to the kitchen and:

3. Depending upon the amount of liquid released from the cooking ingredients, add your home–made vegetable stock,[6] and stir with a wooden spoon, unsticking food if necessary with a wooden spatula. Add and stir in powdered spices. Add in other foods according to the recipe. Put on the lid and ...

   Leave the kitchen to attend to other preparations.

4. Returning to the kitchen:

   Check the liquid; if dry, add vinegar or balsamic vinegar and/ or more stock. Turn off the gas. Grate plenty of parmesan cheese over the food and stir in. Replace the lid and serve. The dish is ready to eat and will stay hot for about as long as it took to cook. The food can even be eaten straight from the pan, best with a wooden dining spoon.

5. Important note:

   Cooking has its many benefits but when time and circumstances does not allow for the recipes found on the following pages, you can still get a good amount of protein, fat, and carbohydrate without having to cook nor resorting to processed cereals or even muesli[7] by having a good few slices of sourdough bread which can be smeared with tahini then smothered with almond, cashew and peanut butters with avocados and tomatoes on the side, followed by some squares of 90–100% chocolate, followed by a smidgin of marmalade on sourdough bread and butter.

PS If you are rushed in the morning, consider installing a breakfast bar, higher than a table, so that you can eat standing up which may even help you digest your food.

---

[6] see Vegetable Stock later on ➤
[7] Cereals on their own have a relatively poor amino acid profile (though improved with added milk) and lack other nutrients like vitamin C.

Breakfast: cast of characters

extra virgin olive oil
tomatoes leeks shallots
parsley dried basil dried marjoram
vegetable stock
turmeric paprika cinnamon black pepper
baked beans
mushrooms
wine or cider vinegar balsamic vinegar
tahini
potatoes
parmesan cheese
unsalted butter
sourdough bread
eggs
anchovy paste
tin of sardines
lemon
cooked greens
alfalfa sprouts

NOW FOR THE DETAILED DAILY
BREAKFAST RECIPES ...

Monday (simplest) breakfast

1. Place your Pyrex™ or CorningWare™ on a small ring. Pour in a dessertspoonful of extra virgin olive oil
2. Light the gas beneath the pan at its lowest setting
3. Add a dozen cherry tomatoes or proportionately fewer middle–sized or a couple of large tomatoes chopped in half or quarters
4. Add chopped leeks if you are using them
5. Add chopped parsley
        [a couple of minutes so far, depending on whether you did any chopping previously] Put on the lid and …

Leave the kitchen for ten minutes or so to get ready for the day or attending to small people or other tasks. Return to the kitchen and:

6. Depending upon the amount of liquid released from the cooking ingredients, add some spoonfuls of vegetable stock and stir with a wooden spoon, unsticking food if necessary with a wooden spatula
7. Add and stir in turmeric, paprika and maybe a *little* cinnamon
8. Put on the lid and …

Leave the kitchen to attend to other preparations. Return to the kitchen and:

9. Stir in a tin of baked beans
10. Add a good fistful of dried basil and stir in
11. If a little dry, add a spoonful or two of wine or cider vinegar
12. Turn off the gas
13. Mix in a few drops of balsamic vinegar
14. Add a spoonful of tahini
15. Grate plenty of parmesan cheese over the food and stir in.

Replace the lid and serve. The dish is ready to eat and will stay hot for a good few minutes.

Tuesday (richer) breakfast

1. Place the shallow casserole on a medium ring
2. Light the gas beneath the pan at its lowest setting
3. Add a dessertspoonful of extra virgin olive oil
4. Add chopped mushrooms
5. Add a dozen cherry tomatoes or proportionately fewer middle–sized or a couple of large chopped tomatoes
6. Add chopped leeks or shallots if you are using them[8]
7. Add chopped parsley. Put on the lid and …

Leave the kitchen for ten minutes or so to get ready for the day or attending to small people or other tasks. Return to the kitchen and:

8. Depending upon the amount of liquid released from the cooking ingredients, add some spoonfuls of stock and stir with a wooden spoon, unsticking food if necessary with a wooden spatula
9. Add and stir in turmeric, paprika and maybe a little cinnamon
10. Add potatoes from the fridge sliced longways in half and stir in

---

[8] Add the leeks to the mushrooms as they start to cook. Leeks fry poorly but braise beautifully.

11. Add a good fistful of dried basil and stir in. Add a good pinch of dried marjoram and stir in.
12. Stir in a spoonful of wine or cider vinegar and two spoonfuls of your stock
13. Squeeze in a length of anchovy paste from the tube and blend into the liquid
14. Crack an egg for each person on top of the food** on to which you can grind some black pepper and a few crystals of salt. Replace the lid.
15. After a few minutes (during which time you can leave the kitchen) the eggs will have cooked, more steamed than fried and will not overcook

Return to the kitchen and, if you are happy with the eggs, turn off the gas. Replace the lid and bring to the table. The dish is ready to eat and will stay hot for about as long as it took to cook. The food can be eaten straight from the pan (though careful not to burn mouths), best with a wooden dining spoon if you have one.

A variant of this recipe with the eggs scrambled is found after the Friday breakfast following on from the page on eggs in general.

**If you want the egg to stay in place and not let it wander over the food, you could create a little well with your wooden spoon and (with perhaps a dot of butter) crack the egg into that. I have somewhere a little ring with a handle (looks like a biscuit mould) which would certainly keep the eggs in their place. Depends how regimented you want them to turn out.

Wednesday breakfast
(a variant on Tuesday)

1. Place the shallow casserole on a medium ring
2. Light the gas beneath the pan at its lowest setting
3. Add a dessertspoonful of extra virgin olive oil
4. Add chopped mushrooms
5. Add a dozen cherry tomatoes or proportionately fewer middle–sized or a couple of large chopped tomatoes
6. Add chopped leeks if you are using them or better still shallots (which peel easily and cook well)
7. Add chopped parsley. Put on the lid and ...

Leave the kitchen for ten minutes or so to get ready for the day or attending to small people or other tasks. Return to the kitchen and:

8. Depending upon the amount of liquid released from the cooking ingredients, add some spoonfuls of your stock and stir with a wooden spoon, unsticking food if necessary with a wooden spatula
9. Add and stir in turmeric, paprika and maybe a little cinnamon
10. Add potatoes from the fridge sliced longways in half and stir in
11. Put on the lid and ...

Leave the kitchen to attend to other preparations. Return to the kitchen and:

12. Stir in a dessertspoonful or two of baked beans
13. Add a good fistful of dried basil and a good pinch of dried marjoram; stir
14. If a little dry, add a spoonful or two of wine or cider vinegar
15. Add an avocado on to which you can grind some black pepper
16. Mix in a few drops of balsamic vinegar
17. Stir all together and turn off the gas
18. Grate plenty of parmesan cheese over the food and stir in.

Replace the lid and serve. The dish is ready to eat and will stay hot for about as long as it took to cook.

Thursday breakfast (with omelette)

1. Place the shallow casserole on a medium ring
2. Light the gas beneath the pan at its lowest setting
3. Add a dessertspoonful of extra virgin olive oil
4. Add a dozen cherry tomatoes or proportionately fewer middle-sized or a couple of large chopped tomatoes
5. Add chopped leeks or shallots if you are using them
6. Add chopped parsley. Put on the lid and …

Leave the kitchen for ten minutes if you need to. Returning:

7. Depending upon the amount of liquid released from the cooking ingredients, add some spoonfuls of stock and stir with a wooden spoon, unsticking food if necessary with a wooden spatula
8. Add and stir in turmeric, paprika and maybe a little cinnamon
9. Add potatoes from the fridge sliced longways in half and stir in
10. Add a good pinch of dried marjoram; stir
11. Put on the lid and …

Leaving the kitchen if you wish, then:

12. Add a good fistful of dried basil to the pan and stir
13. If a little dry, add a spoonful or two of wine or cider vinegar
14. Add an avocado on to which you can grind some black pepper
15. Mix in a few drops of balsamic vinegar
16. Stir all together, replace the lid and turn off the gas

Replace the lid. The dish is ready to eat but will stay hot while you prepare and cook the omelette(s) (see below) unless you made one the night before. Omelette—hot or cold—can be added to everyone's plate or sliced on a plate of its own.

French omelette

This is a dish of eggs seared in very hot (but just off burning) butter. The omelette pan is best not used for any other cooking. It works better if it has low curved sides. The number of eggs depends upon the size of the pan. Mine is steel (to be preferred), ten inches in diameter with sides two inches high and comfortably accommodates one, two or three eggs but would not do so well with four. I once had a beautiful pan with a lipped edge but had to leave it behind and have never seen its like again.

- Place the omelette pan on the large or medium ring. Add to it a good knob of unsalted butter from the fridge. Light the gas and keep on low for the moment.
- Crack the eggs into an old large cup or jug or a mixing bowl (one with a spout is handier). Add salt and pepper and chopped chives and maybe some dried basil. Mix well by hand with a steel whisk but no need to overdo it. Do NOT add water or milk.
- The butter should have softened and melted by now. Grasp the pan handle and swirl the butter around the pan and up the sides so all

is briefly coated. Once the butter has all melted and is bubbling and spitting, TURN GAS UP TO HIGHEST LEVEL and slide the pan around on the fire, swirling the sizzling butter to cover the surface of the pan. It's not too late to add more butter if you think you've been a bit stingy.

- When the butter stops bubbling all the water has burned off, so BEFORE it burns:
- Pour your eggs into the centre of the pan where they will seethe.
- Pull the mass of eggs towards you with a spatula and tilt the pan away from you to allow the liquid eggs to spread in that direction; wiggle the pan about to get the eggs to flow, then tilt the pan back towards you. The eggs are bubbling furiously: liquid on top and hardening underneath. Push the hardening omelette to the far edge of the pan with a spatula and hold it there while you then tilt the pan towards you so that all the remaining liquid egg spreads evenly over the pan. You can turn the gas down to medium or even low now, if you wish.
- When set or almost so, hold the pan tilted onto its side over a cold or warm (but not hot) plate and drop the edge of the omelette on to it and deftly twist the handle so that the bottom of the omelette comes out on top then with a flick of the wrist you finally deliver it folded. [This is the kind of thing U–tube was invented for!] The omelette will be firm on the outside but soft though cooked inside. If the plate were hot, the omelette would keep on cooking and so might then become dry and leathery.
- For this to be a true French omelette, the eggs will have been in the pan for less than 30 seconds. So although it sounds like a lot of drama (and first time it may be: practise at weekends), the whole process from start to finish takes less than two minutes.

Spanish omelettes are different and I suppose more in keeping with the slow cook method but they do need more watching and make washing–up less easy and they take much longer than two minutes.

Further digression on eggs
boiled, poached, scrambled, and braised

This page is for those who, for once, have extra time or who want to vary Tuesday's breakfast or want a change from Thursday's omelette.[9]

Boiled eggs need more attention and tolerate less distraction than is appropriate for these *slow–but–brief* breakfasts. One or two famed cookery writers had the temerity to teach people how to boil an egg which aroused a deal of hostile comment. I can't see why: boiling an egg—which is supposed to be the only thing bachelors can do in the kitchen—is actually quite difficult to get just right because being under-done or overdone comes about all too easily. So it is with poaching.

Poaching eggs in the 'approved' manner needs an awful lot of water (and therefore fuel and time) with variable results, the freshness of the eggs supposedly being a critical factor. My mother possessed an egg–poacher which was supposed to smooth out all these tricky manoeuvres but she didn't use it that often which might tell us something. It was an aluminium pan with a lid and a metal plate on which the three poach-ers sat. It was clattery and not easy to wash up even when you'd but-tered the metal poaching saucers well. Misnamed because they steamed rather than poached. My memory of its product features a rather too solid egg in the shape of a flying saucer perched upon a thick slice of square white toast. It also needed close watching which rather disquali-fies it from inclusion in this book.

One way round this is to follow my own improvisation which only works well if you are also eating avocado (with which poached eggs go well). Boil water in a small saucepan (mine is nine centimetres tall with an eleven centimetre base and a well–fitting lid) on the smallest ring while other food is slow–braising. Slice your large avocado in half and remove the flesh into its destination dish. Float one of the avocado half–husks on top of the water which is barely simmering and crack an egg into it. Replace the lid and leave it to poach and effectively steam. When cooked, the egg scoops out easily onto your food without—unlike metal poachers—sticking to the avocado half–husk. Single use only! It ends up in the company of its other half in the compost bin instead of the washing–up bowl.

---

[9] Choice of day is of course yours to make, not mine! Days are just a numbering conve-nience more friendly than numbers or letters.

The omelette stands alone and bypasses in its own way all these fussy particulars. Otherwise, slow–braising is the method that can include eggs (see Tuesday) but allows you to get on with other things while the food cooks itself.

I do not see the point of using an electrical whisk or whizzer on eggs: you just end up with what I call "startled eggs". Maybe they are good for soufflés, but what do I know about soufflés?

As for scrambled egg, a lot of opinions float on this creamy sooth-ing buttery mixture. In my youth, one landlady—who had insisted I cater for myself—couldn't resist coming into her kitchen in which she thought I had been spending an indecent amount of time—and showing me how to convert my perfect scramble into the leathery curdy mess she thought satisfactory. In theory, scrambling should go well with the breakfast recipes in this book but that is only if you are willing and able to stand over the pan instead of leaving it to cook. So, just for com-pleteness, and assuming you had the time, the following page describes how I would recommend scrambling as a modification of Tuesday's breakfast.

Alternative Tuesday breakfast with scrambled eggs

1. Place the shallow casserole on a medium ring
2. Light the gas beneath the pan at its lowest setting
3. Add a dessertspoonful of extra virgin olive oil
4. Add chopped mushrooms
5. Add a dozen cherry tomatoes or proportionately fewer middle–sized or a couple of large tomatoes, chopped in half or quarters
6. As an additional option add chopped red peppers
7. Add chopped leeks or shallots
8. Add chopped parsley. Put on the lid and let it be for 5–10 minutes
9. Stir with a wooden spoon, unsticking food if necessary with a wooden spatula
10. Squeeze in a length of anchovy paste from the tube and blend into the food
11. Add potatoes from the fridge[10] sliced longways in half and stir in

---

[10] see Resistant Starch later on ➤

12. Crack one or two eggs for each person into a separate bowl into which you add ...
    - ➣ a good knob of unsalted butter straight from the fridge
    - ➣ a good fistful of dried basil,
    - ➣ a good pinch of dried marjoram
    - ➣ turmeric, paprika and maybe a little cinnamon
    - ➣ plenty of freshly ground black pepper
      No salt as the anchovy paste will have salted the food
      Beat all ingredients together into a smooth mixture with a whisk or fork (the butter may remain a bit lumpy, no matter) and then:
13. Pour the contents of the bowl onto the food in your casserole and stir in well with a wooden spoon or spatula. Replace the lid but lift it from time to time to stir further
14. After 4–6 minutes the eggs will have been cooked by steam and contact with the hot food; they will have been entirely amalgamated without being overcooked; they may be barely visible but will enrich the taste and texture
15. Turn off the gas. Replace the lid and bring to the table. The dish is ready to eat and will stay hot for about as long as it took to cook. The food could even be eaten straight from the pan (though careful not to burn mouths), or served separately, best eaten with a wooden dining spoon if you have one.

Friday fish breakfast

1. Place the shallow casserole on a medium ring
2. Light the gas beneath the pan at its lowest setting
3. Open a tin of sardines and pour its oil (if you trust the make) into the pan, otherwise (or as well) add some extra virgin olive oil
4. Add a dozen cherry tomatoes or proportionately fewer middle-sized or a couple of large tomatoes which you have chopped in half
5. Add a couple of thick slices of juicy lemon with skin
6. Add chopped leeks or shallots if you are using them
7. Add chopped parsley. Put on the lid and …

You can leave the kitchen for ten minutes or so. Returning:

8. Depending upon the amount of liquid released from the cooking ingredients, add some spoonfuls of stock and stir with a wooden spoon, unsticking food if necessary with a wooden spatula
9. Add and stir in some turmeric and paprika
10. Add potatoes from the fridge sliced longways in half and stir in
11. Add a good pinch of dried marjoram; stir
12. Put on the lid and …

Leave them to gently cook. When you come back:

13. Add some green beans if you have them, or any chopped cooked cabbage or broccoli
14. Add a good fistful of dried basil and stir
15. If a little dry, add a spoonful or two of wine or cider vinegar
16. Stir all together and turn off the gas
17. Mix in a few drops of balsamic vinegar
18. Add the sardines to sit on top or mix in, as you like.

Replace the lid and serve. The dish is ready to eat and will stay hot for about as long as it took to cook.

Saturday wholefood breakfast

No need to cook if you don't want to. Rather than croissants, I suggest spreading tahini over sourdough bread, covering with alfalfa sprouts then almond, cashew, hazelnut or peanut butter or all of the above. If you have room for a second slice, follow with chocolate–and–hazelnut spread if you can find one low in sugar but you will have your own ideas. I cut and spread the whole lot on a large wooden rectangular board then eat from it so no plates needed.

As for …

Sunday breakfast

You might want to put the whole week's breakfast together and add some artisanal black pudding or, by contrast, just have muesli, yoghurt, blackcurrant jam and banana and look forward to lunch or dinner.

~~~ ~~~ ~~~

Other meals

B reakfast may be the most important meal in a working day but most people won't want it to be the only one, so—after ideas for seven breakfasts—here are fourteen recipes for other meals so that with this book alone you would not repeat yourself in a fortnight. Another reason for having this number of different food types is that some foods—such as liver—are needed once a fortnight for health but might not be good for you, or the planet to eat more often.

All recipes sound complicated—especially roasts—but once you have tried them a few times (and modifying them to suit yourself) they become easy so that, without having to think about it, you have a repertoire of a fortnight's food for yourself and others.

Many of these recipes require onions and carrots, both of which are major ingredients of your vegetable stock, so now is time to show how the making of this essential material is routine and straightforward.

Vegetable stock from your steamer

Steaming pans which hold the boiling water can have a single basket or one or two more nested above them. The boiling water should never actually wet food in the basket—which cooks by the moist heat of steam alone—so the lid needs to be left on during steaming (or replaced by the plates you want to warm). As a guide, water should at least half–fill the pan, and not more than three–quarters. Whenever you steam potatoes or vegetables, the water boiling in the pan will take some colour and nutrients from whatever is in the steamer–pans or colander above.

So from now on it will be the Stockpot.

The first time you use your steamer, the water will have come from the tap and so be clear. If at any time it threatens to boil dry just add more tap water.

When you cook onions, red or white, the outer peel might have to be discarded if it is really filthy but it could be washed and put in the stockpot. The underlying skin and the tops and roots certainly go in, though the roots may need washing a bit if very dirty, but boiling water is a good antiseptic. Other things to go in are the roots and the papery skin of garlic, shallots, parsley stalks, green outer parts of leeks and their roots, but nothing that really belongs in the compost heap. Bay leaves can be added if you have plenty from your tree, so can thyme.

The stock will very soon acquire colour though of course this will be diluted by the water added to keep up the volume. Once it is cool and put in its jug, it goes in the fridge until the next meal requires it. If left out it must be covered.

Carrots are the one vegetable that can be cooked *in* the boiling stockpot water then fished out with a slotted spoon when done to the softness you desire. They will add a good deal of colour and taste to the stock.

The idea behind making your own stock is that 1) your steaming water accumulates nutrients the more vegetables you steam, 2) there are more micronutrients in the bits of onion and other vegetables you discard than in the parts you do eat. So shop–bought Vegetable Stock seems to me an unnecessary extravagance though occasionally I might use some if I am cooking a roast for a number of people and won't have enough of my home–made.

> NB *Beyond lubricating a current meal, I advise against keeping water from boiling (or even steaming) rice or adding it to stock. The same goes for the water in which pasta is cooked.*

Although you can also steam non–vegetable foods, resultant stocks need to be stored separately. I think you will find you will get enough stock from the roast, risotto and stew recipes in this book without needing to steam these foods. Here is an important health message:

> *Store vegetable stock separately from chicken or any*
> *meat or fish stock and keep each of these separate.*
> *Do not combine them in a jug,*

but of course they may be combined in the cooking.

Resistant starch

This is starch that resists digestion in the small intestine and so enters, undigested, into the colon or large intestine where it will be welcomed by the good hungry bacteria of our microbiome. Resistant starch will contribute considerably to anyone's health but especially to those who suffer from abdominal bloating after eating which may stem from bacterial overgrowth in their small intestine. Though the bloating will subside, there may be some odourless flatulence but this will decrease quite soon when resistant starch becomes part of the diet. The additional benefits from an improved microbiome will be better than medicine and almost as good as an expensive probiotic.

White potato provides one of the best and handiest source of resistant starch. This is how you make it: prepare your spuds in your usual way, scrubbing or peeling according to the state of the tuber. Put them in the steamer pan over your boiling stockpot. Large ones are best sliced lengthwise in half or even quarters; smaller ones can be left whole; as you wish, though best if the skin has been pierced in at least one place. Waxy potatoes steam better than floury ones though they do not mash so well if that is what you want them for. Steam them for at least twenty minutes (except perhaps for new season little Jersey potatoes) so they will be cooked right through. *Then let them go cold*. Once they are cold (which is when the starch becomes resistant), you can heat them up again, sauté them or add them to stews or use them in any way you like. It is good to do more than you need at any one time so that, once cold, they can be stored in the fridge ready to be added to your breakfasts. Or they can be brought to room temperature and used as a salad ingredient.

Baking in the oven with just a little oil or butter produces similar results if allowed also to become cold before reheating for eating.

There are other starch–containing foods that when allowed to cool after cooking will liberate resistant starch:

✓ Wholemeal Basmati rice
✓ Pasta
✓ Lentils (a recipe is found on Friday of the second week)
✓ Peas and Beans
✓ Oatmeal (or muesli rich in oats) left to soak overnight, uncooked, in water or milk

Resistant starch has been added to processed food and sold as a supplement on the assumption that because such starch reduces the glycaemic index of carbohydrates, such addition may make Type 2 diabetes easier to manage but the research for such claims is not very substantial. I propose sticking to easily available foods that are simple to prepare.

*NOW FOR MEALS OTHER
THAN BREAKFAST~
A FORTNIGHT OF RECIPES ...*

Sunday ~ roast chicken

For breakfasts, I take Sunday to be the last day of the week but for other meals I put it first because the leftovers spill into the working week.

You will need:

- A chicken that was well–fed and well–treated, preferably from a local farm or smallholding with its
- Giblets
- An unwaxed lemon
- A whole head of garlic
- An onion or two, skinned and roughly sliced
- Bay leaves
- Dried or fresh thyme
- Parsley
- Whole black peppercorns
- Sea salt
- Olive oil
- Vegetable stock
- As many carrots as you like

- Two halves of a sweet potato per person
- Optional extra: a celery stalk or two, roughly chopped
- If you want a dish of white potatoes as an optional accompaniment, put them cold from the fridge [see section on Resistant Starch] into a casserole with plenty of butter also from the fridge and some sea salt. They can cook in the oven alongside the chicken and are nice to serve hot, warm or cold.

Preheat the oven to MAXIMUM. Best results with an electric oven.

Place the giblets in the middle of the pan you are using. I get best results from my large CorningWare™ glass rectangular casserole with lid but the height of these is in the lid not in the pan base so if I am feeding several and therefore want a higher pan wall to contain the extra sweet potatoes and carrots, I shall need my Le Creuset oval doufeu.

Place the sliced onion around the giblets and place the chicken on top, breast upwards.

Stuff the cavity of the chicken with some parsley leaves and stalks, the head of *unpeeled* garlic sliced along its equator, the lemon sliced in half (some juice of which you may with advantage squeeze over the breast of the chicken), a bay leaf or two, some peppercorns.

Chop some carrots or you may prefer to slice a few lengthwise and place them around the chicken on top of the sliced onion; how many carrots depends upon the space left in your casserole. Then put the washed but unpeeled sweet potatoes sliced in half lengthways on top of the carrots and surrounding the chicken.

Pour the vegetable stock (which is best previously heated to simmering point) over the chicken breast until it fills the bottom of the casserole and therefore bathes the vegetables, giblets and base of the chicken. About an inch high is probably about right; the more stock added the more succulent but less crispy the chicken. I plump for succulence.

Sprinkle the breast of the chicken as it faces you in the pan generously with fresh or dried thyme and sea salt and then pour plenty of olive oil over them. Toss in some more bay leaves. Replace lid and put in the oven, noting the time.

After ten minutes turn down to 180°C. After a further ten minutes turn down to 160°C.

After an hour and a quarter from the chicken first going in, check that it is cooked by putting a skewer into the thigh and see that the juice coming out is not pink. Whether fully cooked or not, take it out of the casserole putting it on a plate (or the carving dish to save washing up), then

➤ put the giblets into an oven proof serving dish, keeping them warm,
➤ empty the chopped vegetables into a wide saucepan,
➤ transfer the sliced vegetables (this is where tongs come in)
➤ to an oven proof serving dish and keep warm.

With a roasting fork or whatever ingenuity you can muster without burning yourself or dropping it, hold the chicken over the saucepan allowing all the juices and solids from the cavity to run on top of the chopped vegetables in the wide pan. This is now the gravy saucepan.

A If the chicken was not quite cooked (you saw pink juice), put it back in the oven on its own with the heat turned to 130°C for not more than twenty minutes. Find a way to keep carrots and sweet potatoes warm on their own for now
B If the chicken is cooked, put it back into the now empty casserole, pausing to extricate any veg may have remained in the cavity to enrich the gravy saucepan. Replace the lid and put the chicken back in the oven with the heat turned off for a about a quarter of an hour. It can be joined by the giblets and sliced carrots and sweet potatoes which want to be kept warm but not to keep cooking. Butter and parsley over these sliced orange-coloured vegetables.

While the chicken sits one way or another (as in A or B above), see to the gravy ...

Sauce or gravy

Put a high heat under the gravy saucepan and thoroughly pound and mash all the ingredients. Once boiling furiously, turn down to a simmering and keep mashing. The solids will gradually coalesce with the cooking liquids. When the gravy is still perhaps more liquid than you would wish but is also full of vegetable chunks, remove it (perhaps into a large jug) and pour it through a strainer or chinois back into the gravy saucepan and keep it on a low or medium heat: it will gradually gain a more solid consistency by evaporation. The wider the gravy saucepan the quicker this thickening by reduction will take. A sauce made by reduction this way (which just means reducing the amount of liquid) will preserve taste, colour and texture as well as nutrients better than a gravy made with a highly heated roux. Then comes the question of whether you remove most of the fat from the gravy ...

I have an assortment of gravy fat separators. Some are jugs of ingenious construction which let the gravy out and keeps most of the fat at bay. Others are more traditional china models (also a very good metal one) with differential spouts at opposite ends to hold back or let flow the fat onto your dinner plate.

The fat that will have risen to the top of the gravy in this recipe is nothing more than olive oil and chicken fat. As I like both, I tend to let it be and enjoy a full–fat gravy. However, if this makes the sauce too rich for your taste, separating and removing the fat does have another advantage: you can store it in the fridge and use it to make delicious sauté potatoes at a later date, taking the previously steamed potatoes from your fridge.

If the chicken is ready to carve and the gravy still rather watery even after the reduction and fat removal, it can now be thickened by the addition of vegetables, herbs, powdered spices or other material. These will in any case enhance the taste and texture. But keep the heat down to barely simmering.

Judge for yourself which of the following suggestions go well with which and which less so:

- Dried parsley, basil, tarragon or marjoram
- Mustard powder
  this is the only addition I make regularly plus one or more of the following: powdered turmeric, cinnamon, paprika
- Onion and garlic—cooked in oil on a low heat to almost a paste—is a good, rich thickener
- Almonds or hazelnuts, chopped or ground
- Turnips or swede at least partly cooked (otherwise carrots, but you already have plenty of these in this particular recipe)
- Potatoes crumbled into the sauce then mashed (but avoid all starches from cereal flours except Polenta or even I suppose cooked rice, but that's not my idea of fun)
- The flesh of an apple, well–mashed[11]

---

[11] I mention it as a possibility; I have never actually tried this suggestion I found in *Volaille et Gibier ~ RECETTES SIMPLES VARIEES INGENIEUSES* by Ninette Lyon (Paris 1960). Perhaps I should give it a go.

If you want to thicken with dairy products, take your sauce off the heat and let it cool a bit before you add them:

- Yoghurt or double cream or crème fraîche
- Parmesan or left–over rinds of parmesan
- You could even use powdered milk (if you choose dairy products, they are best added shortly before serving)

In Southern Mexico, Sunday chicken roast is served with three sauces:

- green (from avocado)
- red (from chilli powder)
- brown (from chocolate)
  - ➤ avocado will always be a good thickener for your sauce,
  - ➤ chilli if that is what you want,
  - ➤ but cooking chocolate is very rich and will dominate your other flavours so perhaps reserve it for Easter Sunday
- Also for thickening, you could experiment with yeast extract if you fancy (too salty for my taste) or honey, I have seen a tablespoonful recommended (too sweet for my taste)

Roast food (except for the vegetables) retains its heat for a long time so no need to worry too much about everything being piping hot. Besides, that is one of the functions of gravy: to pour over the cooling veg.

Serve everything up and let those who like them fight over the giblets.

You will need a sharp carving knife and might even invest in chicken secateurs to separate the legs from the rest of the carcass.

I find a metal carving tray with spikes very helpful to secure the bird as it also comes with a gutter to collect juices and jelly from the roast; otherwise use a wooden board.

Have a plate or dish on the table for everyone to discard bones, gristle or anything they don't want to eat. These will go into your chicken stock which will form the basis of tomorrow's delicious supper.

Chicken stock

Put everything from the bone discard plate into your largest pan and fill with cold water which you bring slowly to the boil. While this is happening, slice off any meat left on the carcass and keep in a covered bowl. Any jelly left on the carving plate should also be kept. Make sure you remove the wonderful bits from the base of the bird; the best of these (the oysters) should have been consumed during the meal. When picked clean (but not too thoroughly, every bit contributes flavour and goodness) the carcass joins the bones in the simmering water to which you add a few bay leaves and some dried thyme and even an onion in its skin, sliced in half. Don't at any point add salt. Cover and let simmer on the lowest flame for at least an hour and up to three hours then leave to cool in a cool place before refrigerating. Once the gas is off, it must always remain covered.

Unless you are going to use it very soon, you will need to strain and refrigerate the stock, especially in a warm season. This is where a very large jug comes in handy.

Monday ~ chicken risotto with stock from yesterday's roast

Sweat one or two onions gently in olive oil in at least a medium (26 cms) or a large (30 cms) Le Creuset shallow casserole on a low heat (keeping the lid on) for about ten minutes from the time they begin to gently murmur or even sizzle. A large ring is best if it can be turned down sufficiently low, otherwise on a medium ring. Meanwhile bring your chicken stock gently to simmering point in a separate pan.

Add arborio rice (quantities should be on the packet) to the pan and stir together with the onions with a wooden spoon for a further 5–10 minutes. Now is the time to add one two or three peeled cloves of garlic if you want them. Stir in a little turmeric if you like and don't mind staining your spoon yellow. Add some black peppercorns and a bay leaf or two (and if you like it aromatic, some whole allspice berries[12]). Stir in some dried thyme. Add any jelly you may have salvaged from yesterday's carving tray.

Pour little by little your simmering stock to the pan, something like a spoonful at a time, and stir together with the onions and rice before pouring in the next splash of stock. You could, if you like a bit of saltiness, add an inch or so from a tube of anchovy paste and mix in well.

---

[12] Though I prefer these with lamb; matter of taste.

Cover the pan when all the stock has been added. Don't at any point add extra salt.

Leave to cook gently until all the stock has been absorbed and the rice cooked, which might take about twenty minutes. If it is in danger of drying out, add some of your vegetable stock but no oil or butter. Test a grain of rice which ought to be cooked and still crunchy. When done to your satisfaction, add any left over chicken meat and switch off the gas. If you want to grate any parmesan cheese over, now is the time to do so but the dish is probably rich enough without it. Cover the pan and leave on the warm stove for a further five minutes or so, or until people come to the table.

Needs nothing else though you could have a side dish of peas for people to mix into their risotto and you might follow it with a green salad which you might then follow with a ripe banana mashed into yoghurt topped with cinnamon.

Tuesday ~ Spanish omelette

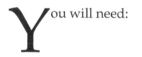ou will need:

- two eggs per person
- extra virgin olive oil
- an onion or two or three, peeled and coarsely sliced
- two or three cloves of garlic, topped and tailed, peeled but left whole
- Herbs: dried basil & dried or fresh thyme, dried or fresh marjoram and/or dried oregano; parsley, preferably fresh
- generous amounts of black pepper from the mill
- sea salt
- as many fresh tomatoes as you like, chopped into large pieces with their stalk insertions cut out (this is the pale disc atop the tomato top)
- one or two red bell peppers cut into chunks with all pith, seeds and stalk removed
- potatoes from the fridge [see Resistant Starch]
- butter fresh from the fridge
- turmeric and paprika

- pimiento (also known as allspice)
- grated nutmeg
- optional extra: some chunks of ham

Sweat one or two onions gently in olive oil in at least a medium (26 cms) Le Creuset shallow casserole on a low heat on a large ring or a medium heat on a medium ring (keeping the lid on) for as long as it takes them to become soft and slightly coloured without browning, usually 10–15 minutes from the start. While they are cooking, beat the eggs into a bowl and add to them the peeled garlic, all the herbs, pepper and salt; also a pinch of turmeric and paprika; mix all well together and leave the bowl stand away from the stove.

Add the tomatoes to the onions in the casserole. Replace the lid for a few minutes to release their juice and soften. Then stir in the red pepper chunks. Replace the lid for at least 5 minutes. Then, stir in the potatoes and a good amount of turmeric and paprika and a very good sprinkling of pimiento (allspice). Replace the lid for a further few minutes. Now turn on the grill so that it is good and hot when you need it.

Take the lid off the casserole and stir everything well with a wooden spatula, scraping any food that might have stuck to the bottom of the pan. Give the eggs and other ingredients in the bowl another brisk stir before adding them to the casserole. Add a good knob of butter (about 2 oz) and some thick chunks of ham if you are having them. Grate in plenty of nutmeg and stir everything very well together. When the eggs start to set, it can be quite helpful to slide a wooden spatula under the food to separate it from the base of the pan. Switch off the gas and put the casserole under the grill to finish cooking the top of your omelette. Replace the lid and bring to the table letting the heat of the pan finish off the cooking and let the food settle for a few moments. Can be cut like a cake and served in slices.

Wednesday ~ green beans
with feta and olives

Take ingredients out of the fridge half an hour before eating. Buy black olives with their stones (pits) intact which will often be from or named Kalamata. They are plump, tasty and delicious. Pitted olives are often dyed black.

Trim the stalk of the beans but you can leave the tips. Steam for 6–10 minutes over your stockpot. Chop them in half if you like and toss them with olive oil, fresh parsley and the feta which you have cut into mouth–sized cubes and a little Dijon mustard and maybe some anchovies.

I prefer to serve the olives separately as its a bit messy to investigate your food for them and allows me to use my oval bowl with its separate ledge to separate the bitten pits from the fruits.

Goes well with crusty bread or add small potatoes to the beans and feta.

Call that a recipe? Probably not.

Thursday ~ ratatouille

One of the advantages of stewing rather than frying courgettes, tomatoes and aubergines in large quantities is that they give you enough soft and delicious material to serve as a sauce, saving you the trouble of making one. This comes in very nicely when, for instance, roasting a chicken in summer.

I use a large Le Creuset casserole, or my oval one which has a larger volume.[13] Though the shape does not match the circular burner, I can't believe that makes any difference given the great conductivity of the metal. If you want a huge amount, use a bigger pot because this dish is lovely cold and even gets better on subsequent days after spending nights in the fridge.

As usual, cover the base of the casserole with extra virgin olive oil warmed over a low heat. First (after topping and tailing them) the sliced courgettes go in.

You can slice them anyway you want but for my preferred method, I hold one end of the courgette above the chopping board with the other end touching it at an angle, then I slice off a piece at an angle then

---

[13] It is marked 26 on the base but this is approximate: at the top of the pan, just under the lid, I measure about 25cms long by 18cms wide.

revolve the courgette in my hand before making the next cut and so on, so that it comes to look a bit like a sharpened pencil. I do the same with leeks. I can't remember from which book I learnt this, but find the pieces more aesthetic than roundels.

Then go in lots of chopped tomatoes, preferably large, but of any shape or size. Then add plenty of chopped fresh parsley. Then put in as many large wedges of onions as you want, perhaps favouring red ones for colour both here and in the stockpot from their tops and tails. Stir then lid on and allow them to sizzle.

Most books tell you to put aubergines first into a colander with salt. It is supposed to remove their bitterness. I have done this perhaps once but now never do as I notice no difference. Maybe aubergines have had their bitterness bred out of them or maybe I just like them as they are. So, assuming that you are with me in having avoided this tedious preliminary, cut off the stalk, slice them in half longways and then cut each half into chunks. Stir them in and around the other two veg and add some bay leaves. One thing certainly true about aubergines is that they absorb a great deal of oil so you might want to add a little bit more as you stir them in, though there is little risk of things getting dry in there with the other fleshy veg giving up their moisture.

After an hour or so, add more fresh chopped parsley and plenty of dried basil and a little thyme and three cloves of garlic peeled but left whole.

What quantities of each? Enough to fill the pot almost to the top. Buy plenty in the summer and then you can have more than one pot on the go.

If you keep the gas at its lowest or (even better) transfer to an oven at 150°C, the pot will need an hour at the very least and can still be happy at three hours. Most recipes use higher heats and shorter times. A Greek version of the dish called Briam (Μπριάμ) adds potatoes from the fridge for the final hour before turning off the heat.

If you are going to finish off with parmesan, best to grate it over each person's bowl rather than the cooking pot as this may be your standby for the rest of the week so best stored without cheese.

Perfect on its own with crusty or pitta bread or, if you didn't add the potatoes, basmati rice. Can keep you going for days in the summer. If it is a winter's night, drink hearty soup (made from stock and onions) instead, followed by cheese and oatcakes.

Friday ~ Salmon with green beans (and samphire in season)

We humans have been able to harvest more food by means of technology than we could by hand and so have maintained and increased our populations. Unfortunately our technical fixes have polluted the oceans so that mercury is now found in most fish. The great benefits of eating fish outweigh the harmful effects of pollution but it still means that it is best not to eat it every day as otherwise might have been advisable in the past. For the same reason, pregnant women might be advised to limit or cut out their consumption during the first trimester. A sad note to precede the cooking of a wonderful food.

You can cook the fish in your Le Creuset casserole on a medium ring with low or slightly raised heat but often, for a change, I use my steel pan with a lid on a large ring with low heat. Either way you stew onions in olive oil until they are soft but not turning dark brown with the lid on the pan, perhaps with a bay leaf or two. Put the green beens or samphire or both to steam. Turn on the grill to high.

Add some white wine or vinegar to the onions and stir in a little thyme or marjoram or both and, pushing the onions aside with your wooden spatula to make a space, put in the salmon—skin side up—after you have added some fennel 'seeds' (they are fruits) or leaf or stem if, like me, you have her growing outside the back door.[14] Replace the lid for a few minutes then look to see how high the colour and texture has altered and softened from the bottom of the fillet. If it has nearly reached the skin (technically the scales), take the pan off the stove and place it under the grill for a minute or two but careful not to make it too crisp. Return it to the stove but switch off the gas, replace the lid and let is sit.

Add, if you like, cold water Atlantic prawns (but not king prawns from warmer regions) and stir them in with the onions. Replace the lid and keep on the warm hob or under the grill with the grill switched off for a few minutes before bringing to table.

---

[14] I find Dill too mild and subtle when cooking fish though it goes well with it cold.

Saturday ~ stewed lamb

Good quality lamb from a local farm cut into more or less equal generous pieces is the starting point from which it is difficult to go wrong. Even if you overcook it, it will be slightly dry and chewy but still delicious and you will know for next time to be gentler with the heat or reduce the timing.

Have some stock or water hot in readiness. Have the oven turned on to maximum.

Stew some onions (as many as you like) in olive oil for ten minutes or so. For this you'll need a round or oval casserole of a size to take the amount of meat you've bought. Add a good amount of tomatoes in season; or mix in a generous amount of sun–dried tomato paste. Add the lamb and, as you stir it in, cover it generously with allspice (pimiento), powdered or whole berries or both.❀᛭ Add some thyme and oregano along with some whole black peppercorns and stir. When the meat has browned a little, cover the contents of the pot with your hot stock; stir then put it in the oven. After a few minutes, turn down to 160°C then let cook for 35–40 minutes at most (25–30 for succulent) then switch off but let the pot sit in the oven for a further 15 minutes. Add more allspice before serving.

Goes well with rice or potatoes (which could have been baking along the stew in a separate dish). Serve with green steamed beans.

Or the lamb could sit on a bed of couscous which could be topped by whole or grated almonds and your rich gravy could be spiced with paprika or even some chilli powder. A good portion of cooked Puy lentils will sit well alongside. [See next Friday's recipe]

❀ variation

Before adding the herbs, you can empty a tin of cannellini or borlotti beans and stir well with the lamb and onions. Before you do so, make sure you not only drain the water from the beans but wash it all out of them very well with running water.[15] This will make a more substantial dish and will necessitate adding 5 or even 10 minutes to the cooking time. The idea is for the beans to blend with the meat and absorb the juices to provide a warming winter dish. Butter beans would go well with the finished dish warmed in a separate pot in the oven rather than being added to the casserole. You wouldn't want both lentils and beans.

---

[15] The liquid in which they were canned but not the beans will give you indigestion.

Sunday ~ roast lamb

Buy a leg or rolled shoulder from your local farmer whose animals graze only on grass and are not abused with hormone treatments or from a butcher who sells such meat, all from a local abattoir. I am fortunate in having two such farms within five miles.

Place the joint in your large glass casserole with lid or Le Creuset oval doufeu on top of a head of garlic which you have crushed to separate and flatten the cloves but have not peeled at all. Toss in some bay leaves and perhaps a sprig of rosemary. A finely chopped carrot and a chopped celery stick can optionally be added.

Rub sea salt into the top of the joint of meat and a good sprinkling of thyme then pour a table spoonful of olive oil over them. Turn on the oven to maximum.

Now surround the lamb with finely chopped onions mixed with a couple of grated cold cooked potatoes, add some red wine or red wine vinegar and some of your vegetable stock and leave all to sit while the oven heats up to maximum. While you wait, place any cooked potatoes (whole or in half) you want to accompany the roast into a separate pot with butter. [See ❀ Variation below]

When the thermostat light goes off at maximum, put in the pot of lamb and the pot of potatoes and let cook for 10 minutes then turn oven down to 160°C then let cook for 40 minutes then switch off but let the pot(s) sit in the oven for a further 15 minutes. The worst you can do is to overcook lamb; these timings depend upon my electric fan oven. The idea is to start very hot because first the cooking pot needs to become hot and then the heat it stores cooks the meat evenly. The vegetables will absorb a lot of this heat and so reduce the risk of overdoing the lamb. Remove the lamb from its onions and place it on a serving dish which you put back in the oven to keep warm in company with the pot of potatoes.

Mash the vegetables and juices in the pan (over a low heat if you chose metal not glass) removing bay leaves and sprig of rosemary. Pick out and discard the skins and roots of garlic but certainly keep the roasted cloves to be mashed in. If there is a lot of fat, pour into a fat separator then reheat what has been de–fatted putting it into a serving jug for use as a delicious lubricant gravy. Some may want to whizz it in a contraption but I like mine chunky or the crudest pieces removed by straining through a chinois. When it is all as smooth as it is going to be, blend in allspice and mustard powders. Serve all accompanied by green peas or with a plain green salad. Carrot and celery sticks can be munched on beforehand along with some olives.

❀ Variation: Before adding the finely chopped onions to the pan, lay a good amount of cooked potatoes in slices, chunks or halves around the joint then cover them with the chopped onions and cold grated cooked potatoes. Then add the wine or vinegar and stock, as before, leaving all to sit while the oven heats up. This saves you the trouble of cooking potatoes in a separate pot. They'll be delicious either way.

Monday ~ improvised with leftovers from yesterday

Planning sounds the opposite of improvisation but "chance favours the prepared mind". You could have ...

- bought more lamb for yesterday's roast than you really needed
- made sure that you kept some of the gravy from yesterday's roast
- done the same for Saturday's stew (which is probably an easier option)
- or all of the above

Whatever you are left with, I suggest the bulk of the meal is carbohydrate in the form of sweet potatoes, white potatoes from the fridge and rice. Now if this were all put together in one dish it would become stodgy and unappetising but simply keeping them apart in separate dishes makes the very same thing attractive.

I would, then, put some sweet potatoes in an ovenware dish. I have two very nice glass ones, one oval the other round, coloured a pleasing red, which are perfect for the job.

- You slice the yams (as they are called in many of the countries from where they come) lengthwise in half. Put them in the dish with a generous amount of butter and parsley and bake them in a moderate oven (150°C) for 45 minutes or an hour.
- Then cook some long grain basmati rice in the way it says on the packet (with bay leaves added to the water if you have them[16]).
- Then steam some broccoli or other greens, and potatoes if your store of them has been depleted. The greens go with the rice, as below.

Pieces of lamb with liquid from the stew or gravy from yesterday's roast or both will mix in with and lubricate the rice nicely, with the cut up lamb providing some solidity and the greens some colour and freshness. The two sorts of potato will sit nicely as side dishes. Radishes on the side or some raw carrot sticks will keep the palate clear. You could add some mustard to where the lamb ends up or just provide a jar of it alongside.

Alternatively, you could blend the lamb with the potatoes of your choice and have the greens mix with the rice separately. A little tahini can help bind the greens with the rice and add some warm flavour.

Improvising means taking a relaxed look at what you have and deciding without any rush as how you would like to combine them.

---

[16] Well, not difficult to have them! Once it gets going in the ground, a tree will keep you in leaves for years. Even one in a large pot will keep giving.

Tuesday ~ beetroot and potato salad

For a quiet uncomplicated evening, this salad is filling and satisfying; you can make it as big or small as you like. I buy organic beetroot already cooked in packs. When I do cook them from fresh, I have to say they taste a little better but those I buy are also delicious. For this sort of mixed salad I use a chunky plain ceramic serving bowl. If the food had come straight out of the fridge, such a bowl can be put the into a gentle oven for a little while. The sliced up beetroot and other foods soon take up warmth from that. By the time it gets to the table, everything is at room temperature.

Add to the warm empty bowl a good dollop of wholegrain mustard, put the sliced up beetroot on top of it. If I have nice tomatoes I slice them in as well. Chop a few slices from the base of a stick of chicory, red or green. When the salad is finally composed, some of the remaining leaves can stick up around the border as decorative food. Their bitterness will aid digestion, their crunchiness provide a special kind of fibre. Cooked potatoes from the fridge next, cut in half. Anchovies are always welcome.

Pour over a good cold–pressed extra virgin olive oil. Grind in some pepper, to state the obvious, and some chopped fresh parsley. Then snip in plenty of chives with scissors. Let sit for a few minutes (perhaps in a warm oven if the ingredients are still a bit chilly) before serving.

You will be comfortably full, but to follow with a little cheese and oatcakes with some walnuts may round off the meal nicely.

Wednesday ~ brussel sprouts with chestnuts and tahini

The sprouts are effectively buds and so contain a huge amount of potential in a small space. If you buy them from a local farmer's market and they are dirty and very manky (rather than cleaned for the supermarket by someone barely gaining a living), no matter: cut off the outer leaves and the inner sprout is perfectly clean. Once you have this green bullet in your hand, slice it in half along its length and put it straight into your cooking pan for which I recommend a Le Creuset round casserole, probably your smallest unless you are feeding many. The smaller sprouts are best left whole.

When the pot is full of sprouts, cut a couple of small onions into fine slices and mix them in with the sprouts. Pour a tablespoonful of oil (olive or rapeseed or both) over them and put the pot on a medium ring on low heat for 5–10 minutes. Have the oven already switched on to maximum.

Then cut or crumble whole cooked chestnuts and add them to the sprouts which will be barely sizzling. Stir in some mustard powder and add a little red or white wine vinegar. Stir well and transfer to the very hot oven. After 5 minutes, turn down to 160°C. After about 40 minutes, switch off the oven. In any case, leave the pot in the oven for a further 5–10 minutes. Then add some tahini if you like along with some balsamic vinegar. Stir everything in the pot well and serve. They go well with cooked turkey or chicken breast, with mango chutney on the side.

If you preferred some hot meat to go with it, try a small thin beefsteak or a fillet of duck or game, perhaps wood pigeon or venison or wild boar. These can be cooked in a covered dish (with some wholegrain mustard) in the oven next to the sprouts towards the end of their cooking time, probably not exceeding 10 minutes or do them separately on the stove where you can watch and turn them. If you do add meat, a side dish of sauerkraut will go well.

Thursday ~ savoury vegetable hotpot

1. Preheat the oven to 170°C. Steam the carrots if that is how you want them [see 4 below].
2. Take one sort of pumpkin (also known as gourd or squash, and for this dish I would recommend butternut squash). Having cut off the stalk, slice it in half longwise. Remove the seeds and all the stringy bits. [These could go straight in the compost but as the seeds have health benefits you might keep them to munch on when they have dried out a bit; you could hurry them on a bit by lightly toasting them.] Put the two halves flesh side up into a casserole dish, preferably oval but whatever is at hand. I like to use my red oval glass casserole for this recipe.
3. Take one or two sweet potatoes per person, and having cut off the tiny stalky bits at each end, slice each in half longwise. Open out the halves and have them join the squash in your casserole dish.
4. Peel two or three carrots per person and top and tail them. They could go into the pot raw but I find they do better if previously lightly steamed. At other times, in other meals, I boil carrots in the stockpot but then they take on the dark colour of the stock which you may agree spoils the clear orangey look of this dish. Whatever you decide

to do with them add them whole if thin or sliced in half longwise if they are large.

5. Take one or two white potatoes per person out of the fridge [see Resistant Starch] and slice each in half longwise. Have all the halves join the squash and sweet potatoes and carrots in your casserole dish.

6. Generously daub the faces of each of the larger vegetables with unsalted butter straight from the fridge. Sprinkle large amounts of coarsely chopped fresh parsley over all the veg. Toss in a bay leaf or two. Put in a few black peppercorns but, to enhance the subtlety of flavours, especially the squash, do not add milled pepper nor add salt. Pour over a small amount of virgin olive oil. Put on the lid and place in the preheated oven and leave to cook for 40 minutes. Take out and stir all the veg. At this point if you want a bit of green to go with the orangey colours, add (fully defrosted) peas now. Put the pot back in the oven for another 10 minutes at the lower heat of 150°C then switch off the oven and let them sit there for a further 5 minutes or so before serving. If you didn't add the peas, you might want some steamed green beans as a side dish.

Side–dish of vegetable in a pot

The recipe above may take longer than so–called stir–fry but I believe you will find it more satisfying and digestible. Many other vegetables baked slowly on their own make an excellent side–dish. A good and underrated example is swede, a vegetable that keeps well before and after cooking.

Just peel away the base and any manky bits that are belong in the compost heap not in the pot. Cut into thinnish slices. Place in a glass casserole and cover with fresh parsley. Pour over them a good amount of organic locally grown rapeseed or olive oil (or both), and put in a moderate pre–heated oven for 45 minutes or so, or an hour from cold. Using glass rather than cast iron saves you troubling with the hob. Delicious hot, or cold with yoghurt. Anytime.

The swede is satisfying (and slightly sedative). Don't forget how good slowly baked vegetables taste, how easy they are to have as food to welcome you home when tired. Always cook more than you need at one sitting so you will have a ready supply of left–overs. The word left–over should have a better connotation. You could almost run a delicatessen on such feasts.

Perhaps this is the place to put in a word for spinach because it can be cooked in minutes. It is (like alfalfa) a good source of vitamins A, E & K but although it contains a lot of iron and calcium these cannot be absorbed because of the high amounts of oxalic acid in the leaf. Indeed large amounts of spinach might leach iron from other foods eaten at the same meal. However, if you cook it in a lot of water and throw the water away, you remove a good deal of the oxalate (and unfortunately also the water–soluble B vitamins).

I like to add cooked spinach to potatoes (from the fridge; see Resistant Starch) that I braise with butter, turmeric, paprika and maybe a touch of chilli powder.

Friday ~ puy lentils with anchovies

Place the lentils in a saucepan and cover them with at least twice the amount of cold water. Pick out the floaters, then bring to the boil, then cook for about 25 minutes, more gently as time goes by, adding boiling water if the pan is at risk of boiling dry. Do not add salt or anything else.

Meanwhile, in a shallow Le Creuset casserole with lid (small, medium or large according to the number of people eating), gently stew a couple of onions in olive oil then, when soft, add a tin of beautiful anchovies, mashing them in with a wooden spoon until they all but vanish (or they will do once you add the lentils) …

Strain the lentils, *not* using what may be left of the cooking water, but of course they'll be wet with it. Add them to the onions, stirring in well. Leave them on a very low flame for about 20 minutes, adding some sage, savory (if you can get this herb) and pepper and a little thyme and at least one bay leaf. Occasionally I add a little paste of sun-dried tomato and some turmeric. A knob of butter towards the end does well, as does some fresh parsley mixed in to cook, also over the food when serving.

Goes well with rice. This dish is wonderfully warming in November and its smoky flavour is good cold in the summer (when it will be a good source of resistant starch. For those who might be averse, does not taste at all fishy.

Saturday ~ liver in the venetian manner

Stew onions in olive oil slowly in a heavy shallow Le Creuset cas-serole with lid (small, medium or large according to the number of people eating), for 25 minutes. Don't fry them: for the whole of the cooking the pan remains on the same low gas.

While they cook, take your time to slice the liver with a razor sharp knife, which you cut into the thinnest slices possible.

At the end of the 25 minutes, stir in a good handful of chopped fresh parsley and perhaps a leaf or two of fresh sage (or a pinch of dried). Replace the lid and cook for a further 3 minutes on the same low gas.

Stir in all the sliced liver and cook for a further 3–4 minutes without turning up the gas, stirring all the while. Switch off the gas and let it sit with the lid on before serving.

Sits well on crushed or mashed potatoes, but not for long.

It is rich, so best eaten on its own, or with a few green beans or per-haps followed by a green salad dressed with mustard and/or preceded by radishes or a little beetroot or pineapple.

~Any time you are tired and want something quick and easy~[17]

There has been no mention of pasta so far in this book. Nice to have occasionally but if used too often out of "convenience" may then displace more nutrient–dense foods. However, we all need some convenience at times so here is a useful standby that includes some greens:

Onto a heated bowl of fusilli (which you have cooked according to the advice on the packet but to the texture you like) mash in:

- Some steamed broccoli, plus:
  - ➢ a few squirts from a tube of sun–dried tomatoes
  - ➢ a generous amount of extra virgin olive oil and
  - ➢ a sprinkling of pine kernels (always good to have some in the cupboard).

This may be quite enough but if you wanted some fish, maybe some tuna from a tin could be mixed in but if you did you would probably do best to omit the pine kernels.

---

[17] When you are tired, don't forget *Side–dish of vegetable in a pot* from last Thursday.

This quick and convenient meal will be comforting as well as nourishing, especially if parmesan is freely grated over the food in kitchen or at table.

Of all the varieties of pasta I find that fusilli keeps the best, cooks the best, absorbs the added extras best and even tolerates a little overcooking.

As for pans, although it is possible to cook pasta in a small pan of boiling water and put it through a strainer when done, the results are usually dismal. If the pan is too cheap it will be too light. I am not recommending you go to extravagant lengths but you will have a more satisfying time if you have a good, appropriately large heavy pan for cooking pasta at a simmer. Maybe to fit inside your usual steamer you could invest in a really good pasta insert. The most expensive pan I own is a large urn-shaped steel pot by Alessi™. The lid alone cost as much as a small pan.[18] A tall perforated insert holds and cooks the pasta. You just lift it out to let the pasta drain, preserving the cooking water[19] and protecting fingers from scalding. It is a thing of beauty but I cook pasta so rarely—now the children have grown up—that it may seem wasted on me, though it still gives me great pleasure to use. It will last generations. But there is surely a middle way and I hope and trust that you will find a pan to suit and serve you for many years.

~Even quicker and easier~

Nobody goes to a book to find out how to make a sandwich (though even sandwiches vary in taste and interest) but I have to mention alfalfa sprouts as a nutritious filling to a sandwich that is a meal in itself and will be appreciated by children.

This assumes you have absorbed the making of alfalfa sprouts into your routine and that you have left some of them to go on to sprout some larger leaves. See below.

For a filling and tasty meal: first slice and finely dice an onion and put in a bowl. Drain a tin of (sustainably caught) tuna fish and add it to the bowl with some cold-pressed virgin olive oil and the juice of a lemon. Fork well together then add some paprika and a good amount of

---

[18] Even if money were no object, I am not sure that steel of this quality is still to be found.
[19] For a short time only; may lubricate a sauce for the current meal. See *Vegetable Stock from your Steamer*.

black pepper from the mill and a splash of balsamic vinegar. (You could add a small amount of yoghurt or cottage cheese if you wanted a creamier result but wanted to avoid industrially produced mayonnaise.) Fork everything together again and let it sit together a few moments.[20]

Spread your mixture onto the biggest slice of rye or wheat bread you can find. Smooth it evenly then cover with alfalfa leaves and then cover with slivers of avocado, finishing off with a good sprinkling of alfalfa sprouts and some walnuts. This open sandwich (if you don't mind the contradiction in terms) is a knife and fork affair. Alternatively, use flatbread to create a wrap.

Alfalfa sprouts

You can buy them already made but they have a short shelf-life and are never so good as your own.

The best way to make your own bean sprouts is to buy a sprouter, which is nothing more than a small stack of two or three perforated trays that fit together with a lid and comes with the very straightforward instructions: it's just a question of watering them everyday and keeping them somewhere warm and moist out of direct sunlight.

The whole-food shop that sells them will probably also stock a good quality of the alfalfa seeds to sprout.

In theory, you could instead use a set of old jam jars with muslin as perforated lids, but in practice these are fiddly and take up much more space.

Your first sprouts will be ready in a very few days and then you just keep them going, harvesting them and making new ones every day or so. They can be added to cooked foods and salads and go well with fish and avocado but many other foods.

In your sprouter, you can let one batch go further to make some leaves for the sandwich recipe above but they also make a pleasant and restorative tea.

---

[20] Even better if you made it earlier or even the night before and left it covered in the fridge.

June

ALFALFA

Rich in vitamins and minerals, alfalfa is a valuable dietary supplement especially for those who need to put on weight. Not only are the leaves good but the sprouting seeds are especially nutritious.

Continued overleaf

ALFALFA

alfalfa
From *The Herbal Year Book* which I wrote for
Eel Pie Publishing in the late 1970s

Satisfaction

Food, water and sleep make up the three essentials for staying alive, companionship being the fourth that makes life worthwhile. Feeling satisfied is one of the purposes of life. Satisfactions are partly learnt: eating is natural and cooking is part of growing up.

Patterns of satisfaction can be cultivated. Dietary choices provide the raw materials for feeling good. Satiety—the sensation of feeling full—is a very complex process that depend upon an interplay between hormones—in the gut and in the brain—and with the anatomical filling and emptying of the stomach. Fats remain in the stomach for the longest time while sugars and starches leave very quickly. Children can and should accommodate a great mixture of foods because they have to grow. So sugars and starches will make up a bigger proportion of their intake than might be helpful for an adult. As well as calories, everyone also needs the full range of minerals and vitamins that come from a mixed range of foods. These will be provided by the recipes in this book.

Children need fats, especially olive oil and some butter. Fats will help them feel fuller for longer and develop their brains. So it is with adults where fats—along with complex carbohydrates and resistant starch—can with benefit make up most of the calorific intake. Fats give more lasting satisfaction than sugars and starches. Paradoxically, a *little* sweetness (for instance in unsweetened yoghurt) at the end of a meal can switch off the urge to eat more by offering the sensation of feeling full.

Favouritism

Isn't this what parents with more than one child are careful to avoid? Toddlers at feeding time notoriously pick and choose, especially if they are given any encouragement to exhibit choice or preference. But, as we mature, isn't learning to like every food to some extent a most useful and adaptive trait as well as being communitarian and cooperative? Besides, enjoying a wide and seasonal range of things is the healthiest of acquisitions. Consumerist individualist culture, very conveniently for the food industry, advocates "favourites" because options that are narrowed and branded favour profits, making toddlers of us all. Online consuming even reduces opinion to Likes and Dislikes. Learning to like and appreciate a wide range of foods must surely be a cultural and health blessing. Variety brings pleasure and tends against the over eating that a narrow diet might favour.

When you cook you become a scientist and an observant experimental technologist. By contrast, when you take food from the freezer to the oven or microwave, you are outsourcing these opportunities.

Cooking food matters

As we need to eat to survive, cooking is necessary work but it is necessary also for good cultural and mental health. A primary skill, it can also be relaxing and give pleasure. Even if children are not always as appreciative as we might like, home–cooking provides them with a memory of tasty food served with care and kindness and a subliminal sense that domestic skills are worth having. These notions will resurface when they settle down.

In Anglo–American culture, we have been persuaded by marketeers that cooking is always a chore, that there are always more important things we could be doing with our time. This from a culture that complains about stress and loneliness with the novel invention of obesity replacing hunger, as if *ever* feeling hungry even for a short while was a perverse affliction. The time saved by outsourcing the cooking of one's own food may be filled by entirely passive pursuits or involve some type of activity, that may be social or solitary or even 'freeing' us to spend even longer hours at work. This will pay for the convenience of someone else's work not in anything like a kitchen but in a factory from where food can be delivered (highly wrapped) to your shop or even your door. Who does it benefit to de–skill a population? Cooking increases personal resilience.

In large towns and cities, especially in warm climates, eating out is congenial, social and relaxing and often inexpensive, but then these cultures may appreciate that those who prepare and cook delicious food are skilled and their individual talents valued. Restaurant culture in Britain is diverse: some has been commodified so that much of the food has been cooked elsewhere, over-salted and heated up on site. Or even taken out of a freezer and transferred straight into a micro–wave. No chance of delicious smells of cooking.

Honest home-cooking remains a selling–point so presumably this quality is valued by customers. I used to love eating out (and used to have to do so as part of my job) but now it is more difficult to find the character of an individual cook in a relaxing and peaceful setting. Some of this longing is a function of old age, but noise pollution and a sense of the frantic helps divert attention away from the food.

Do we really have to be classed as a 'foodie' to enjoy the taste of food over which some care has been taken? Who does it serve to follow a fad or a fashion? Marketeers of novelty for novelty's sake or 'health food' claims. In a culture where anxiety about food and cooking abounds, nutritionism takes hold. The hand wringing and finger wagging of nutritionists along with knowing the twists and turns of the latest scientific research[21] fuels the anxiety.

I have always respected the butcher who buys only from a local abattoir or who slaughters grass–fed animals on the farm; they, and local greengrocers are the true "health–food" shops. Local artisan bakers are making a new appearance in Britain which is all to the good. Grocery has always involved processed foods of one sort or another so the fact that they have been taken over by supermarkets decades ago may even have changed things for the better.

There are, of course, economic and political realities that interfere with home cooking. Cleaners and others who get up early to work for long poorly paid hours may be too exhausted to cook when they return home. At least takeaway food and chilled sandwiches are sometimes of reasonably good quality. It is the industrialised packaged snacks with high salt, sugar and other additives with low nutritive value that pose the greatest threat to health and vigour. People who travel to work and may have more than one employment will want to put their feet up and are unlikely to want to stand for half an hour or more in the kitchen.

---

[21] The research itself can have a shorter shelf–life than some food commodities.

My own experiences have not always entailed short privileged working hours. But even in adverse circumstances, having overcome initial resistance, I have found that carefully peeling onions with a sharp knife is meditative and relaxing. Presumably I inherited this attitude quite unconsciously from my mother, who did take the trouble. Though she kept the house spotless, it has to be admitted that she did not go out to work.

Moralising about people's food choices is condemned as an interference with the freedom to please ourselves. The freedom to remain unhealthy, unhappy and fill the coffers of multinational food corporations whose shareholders surely eat better than those who pay for their unsociable products, whose success in the market depends upon canny and unscrupulous advertising and marketing practices.[22]

All of us belong to at least one culture and culture is largely shaped by food. It would be wonderful to deindustrialise our food so that children will remember the smell from the kitchen rather than the bleep from the microwave. I'm sure I am preaching to the converted.

---

[22] For further reading I can recommend the short and very readable *Why Food Matters* by Paul Freedman 2021 Yale UP.

Foods

Variety is the spice of life but how much variety can anyone comfortably accommodate from week to week, year in year out, From season to season?

It is relaxing to have a full list of foods that are enjoyable and which you expect always to have in stock or to complete your shopping list. Without being rigid, it gives shape to family life without the burden of searching and choosing. When I worked in provincial France, I was impressed by the quality of foods in the weekly market and the local shops but then I was cooked for and that was nearly 60 years ago and things have changed over there. I was, however, struck by the burden placed upon the cook's shoulders; one lady told me in some anguish (and I translate from her Occitan) "Every day, I ask myself, what are we going to eat? What *are* we going to eat?"

So, to minimise any anguish, here is a list that you will supplement or subtract according to your fancy but it is broad and will supply you with all the nutrients and micro-nutrients you need. Taking any supplements with this diet would be completely unnecessary.[23] And, together with the herbs and spices and the *"speedwell"* cooking, it will be delicious and so provide you and yours with the foundation for the good life: simple, relaxing, nutritious, enjoyable food.

Fresh plant foods and fungi

Based upon the observation[24] that eating a minimum of 30 plants a week is essential to good health, I list a few of those that fit in with the recipes in this book with a few extras. Thirty may sound a lot but the point to stress is *diversity*, not quantity: no-one eats a dish of herbs on their own but, added to every meal, they contribute to our intake of plants. So forget the portion size: it is not so much 5 portions a day as many different kinds of plants over the course of a week. You'll score at least a dozen from herbs and spices alone.

Of course any list of foods is arbitrary: there are many other possibilities but all of those listed below are readily available in our shops. Some would cite apples, pears and cherries as their favourite, but, in the end, personal choice prevails; this is my minimum order ...

Almonds	Could you live without them? Like hazelnuts, they make a good flour for making cereal–free cakes. Chewed slowly, a few of these will contribute to general good health.
	If you suffer from cold sores, shingles or any kind of herpes infection, balance a high intake of nuts and seeds (which is high in an amino acid known as arginine) with foods high in an amino acid known as lysine that occurs in: meat, chicken, turkey, peas, tofu, crab, milk, eggs, cheese, spinach and sweet potatoes NB: arginine and lysine are both good and necessary
Alfalfa	See: Bean sprouts

---

[23] With the possible exception of Vitamin D for those who get no sunshine in midwinter or who live above latitude 52°, north or south, where winter sun is too weak to make the vitamin in the skin. Magnesium citrate can at times help asthmatics and those prone to cramp. Nuts and seeds are the major natural source.
[24] Tim Spector *The Diet Myth: The Real Science Behind What We Eat* 2015; *Spoon-Fed: Why Almost Everything We've Been Told About Food is Wrong* 2020. His research with twins shows that our microbiome is even more individual than our genome.

Avocado pears	Not locally sourced but life enhancing!
Banana	Wait until ripe when the skin is spotted black and the flesh creamy. With muesli and yoghurt makes a nutritious alternative to proprietary processed breakfast cereals
Beans	Runner and all green beans are excellent for hypersensitive, allergic people See also: *Tinned foods* below
Bean sprouts	Sprouted legumes: Of these, by far the best nutritionally and offering diverse hormonal and health benefits is alfalfa, known also as Lucerne
Beetroot	They help the heart and blood vessels, tending to lower blood pressure when it is high but not when it is low. They also, like pineapple, help the digestive process in the stomach and small intestine. Being lazy, I buy them organic and already cooked. Make an excellent starter with chives and extra virgin olive oil
Blackcurrant	Excellent source of vitamin C; especially good for hypersensitive, allergic people
Brassicas	Broccoli, Cauliflower, Cabbage, Kale, Kohlrabi, Brussel Sprouts, Chard, Mustard Greens, Rocket, Pak Choi, Radish,Turnip, Swede *Essential to eat from this group every week*
Brazil nuts[25]	Rich source of minerals in principle but now mostly from countries other than Brazil with correspondingly less selenium. [Herpes? See note in Almonds above]
Buckwheat	Not a cereal in spite of the name. Makes wonderful nutty pancakes and also a kind of porridge known as 'kasha' which makes an easy supper with rice. See recipe with Puy lentils (Friday, Week Two)
Carrot	Carotenes are found in all fruit and vegetables of this colour and need to be eaten *at least weekly*
Cashews	Such a convenient and sustaining snack

---

[25] Most of our 'nuts' are actually seeds in the strictly botanical sense but all are highly nutritious.

Chestnuts	Worth making the effort to find them; in Brussel sprout recipe (Wednesday, Week Two)
Chicory	An excellent prebiotic and one I would consider an absolute essential (hence the italics). Add to salad or use the leaves to sandwich finger food, or just chobble on the spears as they are. Keeps better than lettuce. Known confusingly in some countries as Endive, chicory, endive and lettuce are all soporific and very good for the microbiome. Radicchio usually refers to red varieties. The root not the leaf is an adulterant of coffee, which some people actually prefer.
Chocolate	Another bitter vegetable; its greatest health benefits come when the cocoa solids come with hardly any admixture: any chocolate 90% or over will do providing it contains just a little sugar or date syrup but *no* artificial sweeteners. Confectionary below 90% has mixed benefits and below 70% should not be considered as chocolate at all.
Courgette	Good cooked slow; better stewed than fried unless you want an instant summer treat like zucchini quickly fried in butter and oil
Cucurbits	An important family of flowering plants providing medicines as well as food such as: courgettes, vegetable marrows, zucchini; cucumbers, gherkins; squash, pumpkin, gourd; melons, watermelons
Endive	Known in some countries as Chicory; excellent halfway between chicory and lettuce
Garlic	Better roasted or braised than fried; asthmatics are better off with onions, leeks and chives instead
Grapes	Now seedless and tasteless the whole year round but in September seeded grapes from Italy are delicious if you can find them. Raisins make a good occasional snack.
	Good Balsamic vinegar makes all the difference; vinegar from red or white wine or cider is better than cheap balsamic vinegar
Hazelnuts	Make a good flour for cake making. Chewed slowly, a few of these will contribute to bowel health

[Herpes? See note in Almonds above]

Leeks	Versatile; Can be added finely chopped to food as if it were a herb and turn up in some of the breakfast recipes. I used to start with sweating the leeks in oil but they tend to cook to a crisp, as if you had dropped tiny pieces of paper into the food, unpleasant to the mouth, so better added to the already cooking vegetables.
Lemon	Their health benefits need an essay to themselves. Choose ones with unwaxed skin, preferably organic. Suggest pouring boiled water on slices of lemon as a morning drink when the rind will yield up its oil. NB Brush teeth *before* eating lemon (or any food) never within an hour *after* eating
Lentils	An essential foodstuff, Puy lentils cook very well (recipe Friday evening in 2nd week) and I think are the tastiest.
Lettuce	One of the best salad greens; best dressed with Dijon or wholegrain mustard, olive oil and balsamic vinegar.
	Can be cooked with peas in stock if you feel like something warm. Soporific and digestive
Melons	good for gout sufferers, as are leeks, lemon and pineapple
Mushrooms	Chestnut mushrooms keep very well. Add shiitake and maitake when available
Olives	Black with their stones. Food of the goddess
Onions	Absolutely necessary in stews
Peas	Like Broccoli, a good source of folic acid, fresh or frozen
Peanut	A jar of Peanut Butter fills a gap and makes a good immediate breakfast in an emergency as does Almond Butter
	[Herpes? See note in Almonds above]
Pineapple	like beetroot, helps the digestive process in the stomach and small intestine, so quite good to eat some fresh pieces before a meal
Pine kernels	Tasty, crunchy and good for supporting natural immunity and reducing hypersensitivities; nuts and

	seeds are in general less likely to show up in the monitoring of pesticide residues than leaf and fruit
Potatoes	Waxy varieties retain shape and texture, floury ones are more suitable for mash. See section on *Resistant starch*
Samphire	Not as unusual to come by as it used to be. Wonderful with fish.
Sesame	Tahini is nutritious, delicious and handy to use
Shallots	Very good in a breakfast dish see the recipes
Sweet potatoes	A versatile tuber which appears in some of the recipes
Tahini	*see* Sesame
Tomatoes	Eat up to a dozen a day, depending on their size. I keep tubes of sun–dried tomatoes for adding to almost everything during winter months when fresh tomatoes from the south taste of very little and use up a lot of diesel getting here; hothouse fruit from the low countries, though, are often palatable
Walnut	A few of these go a long way and may irritate those prone to mouth ulcers. Delicious for the rest of us [Herpes? See note in Almonds above]

There are of course many other plant foods but this is not an encyclopaedia of food and the idea of this book is not to overburden the reader with choice. How many recipes does a person really need? The idea is to have a dozen or two meals that will become easy to cook without having to think about it.

Essential culinary herbs — fresh or dried — and dried spices

I have left out some common herbs because of their potentially undesirable oestrogenising effects. Most spices are important sources of trace minerals.

Allspice	Good with stewed lamb. Also known as pimiento
Bay Leaf	If you plant a small tree, you can harvest gently almost immediately; within a year or two it will produce more than you can use
Basil	Add dried to most cooked breakfasts

Celery	For flavour more than nutrition, if you like it, but has some benefits for metabolism; so less of a vegetable and more of a herb. Good for gout sufferers
Chervil	Lovely delicate herb if you can get it fresh but dry is better than nothing. Goes especially well with eggs.
Chives	Go well with both beetroot and eggs. Snip them fresh into food with scissors
Cress	A brassica good for adding to salads and sandwiches
Ginger	Makes a good tea and can be grated onto food as liked
Marjoram	Goes especially well, fresh or dried, with potatoes, mushrooms and eggs
Mustard	Can be added to food or sauces as a powder or, as Dijon mustard from a jar into salad dressing
Nutmeg	Good with eggs; grate into almost anything you fancy
Oregano	Stronger the further south and higher up it is grown
Paprika	Never be without! Features in most of the breakfast recipes
Parsley	Keep fresh parsley always in the fridge; chop or snip into almost everything. Dried is also very good for all your slow–cooking including stews.
Peppercorns	I have had my mill for 30 years and it shows no sign of wanting to retire but I am not sure if genuine William Bounds are still made: they grind against the pepper not against metal and so "never" wear out
Rosemary	the leaves or a sprig make a good morning tea if you need perking up and can be added to fatty dishes
Sage	as for rosemary; less stimulating but more oestrogenising; a good digestive
Stinging Nettle	Useful as a tea and can easily be picked fresh with gloves (but not after the end of June when they lose their benefit and gain some disadvantages). They can also be cooked for a few minutes (without adding water) like spinach. Picked in spring and early summer they can be easily dried in a warm, dry room or kitchen, out of direct sunlight
Thyme	Dried thyme enhances every stew and a pinch can go into many cooked breakfasts
Turmeric	Features in many of the breakfast recipes

Coffee, tea and other beverage plants

We in temperate regions have become accustomed to drinks made from tropical plants to the extent that some of us cannot imagine life without them.

Coffee has many health benefits but—because of its hormonal and stimulating effects—is best consumed before two o'clock in the afternoon.

The advantages of tea has perhaps a wider profile than that of coffee and most people can take larger amounts without being overstimulated.

These are health plants and consuming appropriate amounts of either or both on a daily basis will provide many benefits as long as they are not taken on an empty stomach because their effect on our blood sugar is only helpful if we have recently eaten. Tannins in tea may reduce our uptake of protein, so like coffee is best not taken when we are eating a meal, though it goes very well with a snack, especially at teatime!

Tea and coffee, like the spices are important sources of trace minerals such as manganese.

Other drinks high in caffeine—such as Maté—are consumed in many countries but have not quite gained international appeal. Chocolate is more of a food than a drink; drinking chocolate or cocoa has much of the nutritious fat removed to make it less bitter and more water–soluble. The preparation from the original seed or leaf of plants usually involves fermentation. To say that alcoholic drinks lie outside the scope of this book sounds a bit prim, even censorious, but I do hope that my readers appreciate the health benefits of a glass of decent wine.

Cereals

Bread   Sourdough is one of the more digestible wheat–breads and so better for the health of your digestive tract: the slow proving of the yeast and dough influences the presentation of gluten to the gut. Helpfully, it promotes more thorough chewing (as does Rye–bread) and so gets digested by saliva in the mouth and then by acid in the stomach before it gets near the small intestine whose lining is sensitive to gluten. Spelt bread has a satisfying close–grained texture though this makes it (like Rye–bread) not so good at mopping up juices and sauces.

Baked goods:	best to limit intake of other baked goods, delicious as they are, more especially biscuits, cakes and pastries if they are industrially produced [see final page]
	Flour added to food burdens our digestion
Durum wheat	Pasta is nice to have occasionally as a "convenience food" taking care that it is accompanied by and not displace more nutrient–dense foods. The same could be said for couscous: very convenient when bought pre–steamed
Barley	Like oats, can reduce blood cholesterol if taken regularly as flakes in muesli or from time to time as barley water but its insoluble fibre can cause abdominal bloating in susceptible individuals. Most muesli contains barley, wheat and oats at least
Muesli	More digestible when softened with boiling water (rather than hot milk) and then eaten when cooler with yoghurt with fruit such as banana or blackcurrant or apple or nuts and seeds
Oats	oatcakes make an excellent contribution to health, going very well with cheese or herring or in muesli or cooked as porridge

Polenta also known as Maize or Cornmeal

As it contains no gluten, cornbread has quite a different texture to breads made from wheat and rye;

there is also tortilla, the flatbread from Mexico

Polenta makes a very good accompaniment to fish, meat and seafood. It also takes up the zest and juice of fresh lemon and orange to make a wonderful almost savoury cake that goes very well with yoghurt and blackcurrants on a summer afternoon

Rice	Basmati rice is the most reliable for good eating and successful cooking
	Of the three varieties readily available for risotto, arborio is perhaps the most versatile, the others being Carnaroli and Vialone Nano (which has the benefit of being able to absorb more liquid)
Rye	See Bread above; like oatcakes, thin slices of rye bread go very well with herring rollmops

Tinned and bottled foods

Anchovies	Essential ingredient to a healthy diet, in tins or small bottles. Anchovy paste is handy to add to many dishes.
Bottled sauces	With your delicious sauces made from the methods in this book, there really is no point unless you want an occasional squirt of Lea and Perrin's to save you a few moments time
Baked beans	In tomato sauce is a great standby. Just about escapes classification as a processed food but read the ingredients very carefully for artificial or even "natural" sweeteners of any kind.
	Cannellini beans make a good accompaniment to lamb. Make sure to drain them of the liquid in which they were canned and rinse the beans in plenty of cold water.
Sardines	Three tins a week of whole fish (not fillets) would provide about the best source of calcium and essential fatty acids. Better in olive oil or brine rather than tomato sauce

Soups

I cannot bring myself to recommend them though I notice that some are better than others such as those that contain sodium alginate from seaweed rather than starch emulsifiers, nor can I pretend that I make my own (though it is about the easiest thing to do in the kitchen). There are some good chilled soups which have few if any additives and you can buy soup in pouches which at least do not contain the emulsifiers which so interfere with the good bacteria in our colon. Powdered soups to rehydrate? Never!

Dairy foods

There are two potential problems with consuming milk: 1) sensitivity to its various proteins 2) the loss after infancy of lactase, the enzyme that splits milk sugar (lactose). Most European populations benefit from lactase persistence. Those who lost the enzyme, suffer only mild, transient diarrhoea if they consume lactose.[26] Whatever the case, drinking large quantities of milk may not be the best form of dairy food: the majority of pastoral peoples rarely consume it straight from their animals. Rather they consume it in some fermented form.

These—like yoghurt and kefir—are excellent and help our microbiome produce their useful metabolites. They can be added to so many foods and are good to eat most days.

Butter and cream

This sumptuous food reduces anxiety and is one of the great blessings bestowed on us by our pastoralist ancestors. My preference favours unsalted butter from Normandy. Seared very briefly in omelettes; otherwise best braised or stewed, not fried. Or plastered onto bread. Butter contains very little lactose and even this tiny amount has been removed from clarified butter or ghee. As for cream, Single contains a lot of milk while Double does not. For other creams, read the label for additives.

Cheese

This food predates recorded human history and is an excellent source of calcium and protein. Cheese from the milk of water buffalo, camels, donkeys, goats, sheep, cows is to this day made on every continent from Chile to Mongolia and Tibet. The proper appreciation of cheese that is made with skill and love belongs with a slow meal and not inside a sandwich.

Parmesan has already been mentioned as an essential ingredient to the recipes. If you buy a shard from an authentic wheel and not an industrially produced lookalike, you will have one of the most nutrient–dense foods available anywhere. Do you really need to have someone in a factory to grate it for you? Feta makes a most versatile snack.

As cheese lacks fibre, it is best eaten with a leaf or stick of chicory or with a starchy food such as oatcakes or bread. Which cheese you choose is of course a matter of personal preference but I would strongly recommend upland or even mountain hard cheeses on account of the mixed pastures and herb meadows on which the animals graze, sometimes in cleaner air. This might come from the Basque Pyrenees; Italian, Swiss or

---

[26] From the work of Richard Evershed, Professor of Biogeochemistry at Bristol and research conducted by his Organic Geochemistry Unit in collaboration with UCL.

French alps, such as *Fior Delle Alpi* from raw milk as well as the better known ones, and a properly designated aged Manchego from La Mancha in Spain. I share with Wallace (of Wallace & Gromit) the choice of Yorkshire Wensleydale as a superb English upland cheese. Then there are the wonderful soft cheeses from unpasteurised cow's milk such as Comté, Brie de Meaux, Epoisse, Roquefort, Camembert. Blue cheeses: the creamy Gorgonzola, the sharp Stilton. When I passed through Gouda in the Netherlands on the train, I did not see a single cow. The lady in the seat opposite said that while most of it was produced industrially the authentic aged, traditionally produced cheese could still be found, as can aged Cheddar.

~~~ ~~~ ~~~

There are so many good things and we are especially blessed in being able to obtain and enjoy them. It does no-one any good to bang on about so–called "bad" foods. Such bad–talking generates a sense of threat instead of the blessing we should be celebrating

But I am going to end on a sour note. In what follows, you will find me bad–mouthing materials that do not perhaps, in every case, deserve the name of food ...

Foods that should definitely be avoided by probably everyone

Most foods provide some benefits. Fibre in plant foods are essential to feed our microbiome which is why eating thirty varieties of plant in a week will keep you well because it is now known that we live in an obligatory symbiosis with the microbes in our guts. These are promoted by fibre and substances in plants called polyphenols which promote our cardiovascular health.

The following foods lack these substances. In failing to provide us with them, these industrialised materials reduce the number of good bacteria and inhibit their metabolic products so that instead of promoting our cardiovascular health they might even initiate heart disease in at–risk individuals if they were to eat little else ...

- Processed meats such as charcuterie, (salami etc), chorizo, bacon

  in small doses occasionally these at least provide nutrients and can be very enjoyable but with constant dietary intake they would make a very negative contribution to health, more for the additives they contain than for the nutrients they lack. Usually they come from industrialised food production; moderate amounts of artisan or home–cured ham may at least on occasion provide great pleasure and this is one of their benefits

- Packaged processed foods or precooked meals

  Emulsifiers and other additives in nearly all processed food may be classed as "safe" because they have not been shown to cause direct harm but should be avoided as they interfere with the good microbes in our guts as do the antibiotics fed to industrially produced meat and poultry

  Foods like nut–butters if made by a responsible wholefood manu-facturer should not contain additives to prolong shelf life and so can be eaten with gusto

- Any kind of sweetener

  whether "natural" or not will tend to disturb our metabolism and very quickly generate poor control of blood glucose and insulin

  The resulting disordered glycaemia will certainly lead to impaired function and exacerbation of diseases associated with ageing

~~~ ~~~ ~~~

Nutrients

Deficiencies are endemic in poverty–stricken countries which is shaming to us all but in countries like ours where being well–fed is available to all but the poorest[27] as a personal option, dietary intake provides the natural and obvious solution. The recipes in this book hopes to suggest how that might simply be achieved.

There are, however, medical conditions of malabsorption that result in deficiency but these are not as common as various cultural fabulists are eager to maintain. To the person who suffers from malabsorption, their signs and symptoms make themselves known only too well.

Aside from such conditions, the human body has had to adapt to minor temporary deficiencies over the millennia when food supply could not have been guaranteed.

An important exception is the complex absorption of vitamin B_{12} which depends upon several factors, notably an intact stomach lining able to produce and withstand good amounts of acid.

---

[27] Yes, I know: it's complicated and not just a question of money.

For growth and maintenance we need five classes of macronutrients:

1. A daily supply of varied proteins with a full range of complementary amino acids which a mixed diet readily provides.
2. While proteins provide us with all our structural materials, we need a regular supply of carbohydrate as fuel. Otherwise we might burn the proteins, which would be a bit like throwing the furniture on the fire to keep warm!
3. Fatty acids found in fats and oils to make and protect our cells and organs, also to manage inflammation and other processes. Olive oil provides a particularly beneficial range of such acids. Lipid is the generic chemical term for fats and oils. Without fats we could not have the fat–soluble vitamins.
4. plant fibre
5. and water

Life also depends upon the two classes of micronutrients:

1. a regular dietary supply of vitamins
2. and minerals

All these are essential, not just desirable.

Like the proteins and fats, vitamins and minerals are intermingled in the foods we eat as it is in all living organisms because life is not compartmentalised. Most vitamins are not single substances but groups of related compounds.

This is a cookbook which claims to promote healthy eating so, in the spirit of providing information to back up such claims, this appendix is going in for some temporary compartmentalisation and will list the vitamins (which are separated into those that occur in fatty foods and those that dissolve in water) and then the minerals so that the cook can check that what they are eating is as healthy as it tastes.

Vitamins

The four fatty vitamins (which can be stored) are named as follows:

Name	Necessary for	Found in
A	1. growth and development of the embryo 2. maintenance of the immune system 3. vision	Two forms: *Retinol* only in animal-sourced foods, such as oily fish, liver, cheese and butter. *Carotenoids* (in orange and yellow plant foods but also dark leafy greens) need to be converted to Retinol
D	Permits calcium absorption, so: formation and maintenance of bone and teeth but many other metabolic functions More a hormone than a vitamin	Exposure of the skin to UVB radiation from sunshine Also in oily fish; and in mushrooms exposed to sunlight, and in fortified foods
E	Antioxidant and probably for healthy metabolism of smooth muscle	Oils from nuts and seeds including wheatgerm and avocado; small amounts in seafood and butter; tiny amounts in other animal foods
K	1. Coagulation of blood 2. Formation and maintenance of healthy bones by calcium salts but also protects against calcification where undesirable, for instance in blood vessel walls	primarily in leafy green vegetables, also in hazelnuts, olive oil, tomatoes, potatoes and some fruit; another form in eggs, poultry, butter, cheese and milk; made also by bacteria which depend upon plant fibre in healthy guts and can be augmented by fermented foods

Now for the water–soluble vitamins, nine in number: vitamin C and eight compounds that together make up what is known as the B complex because some of them are necessary to others. The B vitamins work together to help conduct a very wide range of cellular processes.

For a substance to be called a vitamin, it has to be essential to human life and one that we cannot synthesise and so must consume. The numbering of the B vitamins shows some gaps because it was eventually found that some of them (for instance choline which used to be named B_4 or inositol, the former B_8) we could actually make for ourselves. These and others we can only make in small amounts which explains why some folk consider them worth taking as supplements.

Here is a summary of dietary sources of the water–soluble vitamins:

- Thiamine (B_1) is found in whole unprocessed grains.
- Riboflavin (B_2) is highest in liver; also occurs in dairy produce, almonds and mushrooms. Cereal products are usually fortified with it.
- Niacin or nicotinic acid (B_3) is found in yeast, meat, peanuts, fish (notably salmon and tuna) and in some parts of poultry, mushrooms, tahini and avocado.
- Pantothenic acid (B_5) is found at least in some quantity in pretty much every food. Highest in dairy produce and eggs. Potatoes, tomatoes, oats, alfalfa, sunflower seeds, avocado and mushrooms are good plant sources as are whole grains but most of the vitamin is lost in the milling of white rice or white flour.
- Vitamin B_6 refers to a group of half a dozen related compounds, notably pyridoxal and pyridoxine. Highest amounts in meat, fish and poultry. Although plants contain so much less, research indicates that vegetarian diets are not deficient in this vitamin so presumably the microbiome compensates or absorption pathways adapt, or both. What is eaten is not always what is absorbed or utilised in the body.
- Highest amounts of Biotin (B_7) are found in liver, eggs, peanuts, sunflower seeds, salmon, almonds and avocado.
- Folate (B_9) is derived mainly from plant sources. The vitamin is sensitive to high heat and leaches easily into water which is one reason why most vegetables should be steamed rather than cooked in boiling water.

  Highest in peanuts and sunflower seeds, and other nuts and seeds but good amounts in brassicas, avocados, bread and potatoes.

Highest animal sources are chicken liver, eggs, salmon, milk, yoghurt, butter and some cheeses but this is primarily a vitamin obtained from green plants.

- Blood cell formation and normal nervous system activity depend upon cobalamin or vitamin B_{12}. Plants have no need for it so it is made only by animals and sea creatures; we get it by eating them.

    B_{12} operates with Folate to permit cells to divide and so rapidly dividing cells such as red blood cells are vulnerable to deficiency. DNA cannot replicate without Folate and B_{12} *both* acting together.

    The absorption of vitamin B_{12} is complex, depending upon several factors, notably an intact stomach lining with good amounts of acid, a state we cannot take for granted, especially as we age. So drugs reducing stomach acid are liable to compromise intake of this vitamin.

    An autoimmune disease which attacks those cells and function of the stomach lining that allow the absorption of this huge molecule leads to a condition known as pernicious anaemia. The treatment is intramuscular injection of the vitamin.

- There is only one vitamin C—Ascorbic acid—so we are spared the numbers. Fruit and vegetables provide the principal source.

This is not a medical textbook but it is worth stressing that all the vitamins work in concert which a mixed diet best provides. Vitamin supplementation is therefore a medicinal not a dietary act. The vitamins can only work in the presence of a number of minerals.

Minerals

These are mostly metals that animals, plants, bacteria and fungi have coopted to fulfil their fundamental metabolic needs. We get ours from them and also from drinking water.

The major metals (calcium and iron), being potent, are very cautiously absorbed in case the body should be overwhelmed by them. Better to eat them continually in food because they are needed continually: for bones and teeth, blood and skin and for the maintenance of correct body fluids. They also permit nerves and muscles to work and extract from food the energy we need. Not on their own, though: they need others in the cooperative enterprise that is human physiology: such as magnesium.

Sodium (as in table salt) and potassium maintain the blood volume within tolerable limits and nerves cannot fire without them.

Without the salts of metals such as chloride and phosphate we could not make bones or stomach acid nor would our muscles be able to utilise energy. A couple of the twenty or so amino acids contain sulphur so we need a supply of that element.

Other elements are needed in smaller quantities, because they take part in fewer reactions, so are used up more slowly but are still crucial to normal functioning. They include zinc, copper, manganese, molybdenum, chromium and selenium. Some elements—like iodine—have a single function and so may take weeks or even months for a deficiency to take effect. Iodine is found only in or near the sea or soils that once were seabeds.

Then there are other ultra–trace elements about which there is not even international agreement as to whether they are essential and if so in what quantities.

The major sources of the major minerals are found in fish, seafood, milk products food and meat, fruit and vegetables, nuts, seeds, and pulses.[28] So I think I've got you covered.

---

[28] Just to be pedantically botanical for a moment: many foods we call nuts are seeds while some seeds, such as sunflower and fennel, are technically fruits; as are olive and avocado. True nuts, such as hazelnuts, are fruits that happen not to be fleshy. The fleshy part we eat of an apple is part of the parent tissue so, strictly not a fruit: that is in the core which contains the seeds and is often discarded. We refer to the various fruits and seeds of the bean and pea family as pulses. The seed is the newborn generation protected, fed and dispersed by its parental genetic covering that we call the fruit.

Macronutrients

As essential as these minerals are, we need them in tiny quantities compared to the four major elements: carbon, oxygen, hydrogen and nitrogen. The macronutrients—proteins, lipids, and carbohydrates—are made from just these four elements.

Proteins are chains of amino acids folded in innumerable formations that give us structure but also the enzymes which make living systems possible.

Lipids are constituted largely of fatty acids or related compounds that also have hormonal and enzyme–like activity without which our immune and reproductive systems just would not work.

Carbohydrates (known chemically as saccharides) are found in sugars and starches but also in cellulose and other compounds. They give us energy but those we cannot digest give us the fibre on which our microbiome is entirely reliant. Seafood and mushrooms have cell walls made from polysaccharides that complement cellulose fibre from plants in most important ways.

Printed in the USA
CPSIA information can be obtained
at www.ICGtesting.com
JSHW042155270224
58181JS00010B/83

9 781801 521369